Outdoor Pizza Oven Cookbook

365 Days of Easy & Delicious Homemade Classic Pizzas Recipes, The Ultimate Guide for Beginners to Perfect Pizza Making, and Indulge in the Unique and Irresistible Taste

Blowen Cellehan

Table of Contents

INTRODUCTION

This book is a comprehensive guide to the art of pizza making, focusing on the creation of perfect dough and the exploration of various types of pizza recipes. Whether you're a novice home cook or an experienced chef, this book will provide you with the knowledge and techniques to create delicious pizzas that will impress your family and friends.

The first section of the book delves into the secrets of making the perfect pizza dough. It covers the basic ingredients required, such as flour, water, yeast, and salt, and provides detailed instructions on how to combine them to create a soft and elastic dough. The book explains the importance of kneading the dough properly to develop gluten, which gives the pizza its characteristic chewy texture. It also offers tips on proofing the dough to achieve the ideal rise and flavor.

Once you've mastered the art of dough making, the book takes you on a journey through various types of pizza recipes. It starts with the classic Margherita pizza, which showcases the simplicity of a few high-quality ingredients like fresh tomatoes, mozzarella cheese, and basil. The book explains how to achieve the perfect balance of flavors and textures in this timeless favorite.

From there, the book explores a wide range of pizza styles, including Neapolitan, New York-style, Chicago deep-dish, and Sicilian. Each style is accompanied by detailed instructions on how to shape the dough, the ideal baking temperature and time, and the recommended toppings and seasonings. The book also provides variations and suggestions for customizing each style to suit your personal preferences.

In addition to traditional pizza recipes, the book introduces innovative and creative options for those looking to experiment with flavors. It includes recipes for vegetarian and vegan pizzas, showcasing a variety of fresh vegetables, plant-based cheeses, and flavorful sauces. It also explores the fusion of different cuisines, such as Mexican-inspired pizzas with salsa, guacamole, and jalapenos, or Mediterranean-inspired pizzas with feta cheese, olives, and sun-dried tomatoes.

To complement the pizza recipes, the book offers a selection of delicious side dishes and dipping sauces. It includes recipes for garlic knots, cheesy breadsticks, and a variety of homemade sauces like marinara, pesto, and barbecue. These accompaniments elevate the pizza experience and provide additional options for serving and entertaining.

Throughout the book, you'll find helpful tips and tricks that will enhance your pizza-making skills. It offers guidance on selecting the right type of flour for different pizza styles, troubleshooting common dough issues, and achieving the desired level of crispiness in the crust. The book also provides suggestions on pairing pizzas with wines, beers, and other beverages to enhance the overall dining experience.

Whether you're looking to recreate the flavors of your favorite pizzeria or explore new and exciting pizza combinations, this book is your ultimate guide. With its detailed instructions, creative recipes, and expert tips, it will empower you to become a master pizza maker in your own kitchen. So grab your apron, roll up your sleeves, and get ready to embark on a culinary adventure that will delight your taste buds and impress your loved ones.

Pizza is a versatile and beloved dish that can be customized to suit a variety of tastes and dietary preferences. While it's often associated with indulgence, there are several tips and tricks you can employ to make your pizzas not only more delicious but also healthier. By making mindful ingredient choices and employing smart cooking techniques, you can enjoy a guilt-free and nutritious pizza experience.

One of the first steps to creating a healthier pizza is to focus on the crust. Traditional pizza dough is typically made with white flour, which lacks the nutritional benefits of whole grains. To make your pizza crust more nutritious, consider using whole wheat flour or a combination of whole wheat and all-purpose flour. Whole wheat flour contains more fiber, vitamins, and minerals compared to refined white flour, making it a healthier choice. You can also experiment with alternative flours like almond flour or cauliflower crusts for a gluten-free or low-carb option.

Another way to boost the nutritional value of your pizza is to load it up with a variety of colorful vegetables. Vegetables not only add flavor and texture but also provide essential vitamins, minerals, and antioxidants. Opt for a rainbow of vegetables like bell peppers, tomatoes, spinach, mushrooms, onions, and

zucchini. You can sauté or roast the vegetables before adding them to the pizza to enhance their flavors. Additionally, consider adding fresh herbs like basil, oregano, or thyme for an extra burst of freshness.

When it comes to cheese, moderation is key. While cheese adds richness and flavor to pizza, it can also be high in saturated fat and calories. Instead of piling on excessive amounts of cheese, opt for lighter options like part-skim mozzarella or reduced-fat cheese. You can also experiment with flavorful alternatives such as feta, goat cheese, or even vegan cheese options made from nuts or plant-based ingredients. Using less cheese or spreading it out evenly on the pizza can help reduce the overall fat and calorie content.

Sauce is another component of pizza that can be made healthier. Traditional pizza sauces are often high in sodium and may contain added sugars. Consider making your own sauce using fresh tomatoes, herbs, and spices. This allows you

to control the amount of salt and sugar in the sauce. Alternatively, you can use alternatives like pesto, olive oil, or even a light drizzle of balsamic glaze for added flavor.

To further enhance the nutritional profile of your pizza, consider incorporating lean proteins. Instead of using processed meats like pepperoni or sausage, opt for grilled chicken breast, lean turkey, or even plant-based proteins like tofu or tempeh. These options provide a good source of protein without the excess fat and sodium found in processed meats. You can marinate the proteins in flavorful herbs and spices to infuse them with extra taste.

Cooking techniques also play a role in making your pizza healthier. Instead of deep-frying or pan-frying the pizza, opt for baking or grilling. Baking the pizza allows for a crispy crust without the need for excessive oil. Grilling the pizza adds a smoky flavor and can help reduce the overall fat content. If you're using a traditional oven, preheating a pizza stone or a baking sheet can help achieve a crispier crust.

Lastly, portion control is essential when it comes to enjoying a healthier pizza. It's easy to overindulge, especially when faced with a delicious homemade pizza. To avoid overeating, pay attention to your portion sizes and pair your pizza with a side salad or a bowl of vegetable soup. This helps increase the overall nutritional value of your meal and provides a balanced plate.

In conclusion, making your pizzas more delicious and healthier is possible with a few simple tips and tricks. By choosing whole grain crusts, loading up on colorful vegetables, opting for lighter cheeses, making homemade sauces, incorporating lean proteins, using healthier cooking techniques, and practicing portion control, you can enjoy a guilt-free and nutritious pizza experience. So get creative in the kitchen, experiment with different flavors and ingredients, and savor every bite of your delicious and healthier homemade pizzas.

The pizza oven is a fantastic tool for achieving that authentic, wood-fired taste and texture in your homemade pizzas. Its high temperatures and even heat distribution allow you to create crispy crusts, perfectly melted cheese, and smoky flavors that are difficult to replicate in a conventional oven. Let's explore the various uses of a pizza oven and how it enhances your pizza-making experience.

• Baking Pizza:

The primary purpose of a pizza oven is to bake pizzas. The intense heat generated by the oven quickly cooks the dough, resulting in a crispy crust with a slightly charred, smoky flavor. The even heat distribution ensures that the entire pizza cooks evenly, from the crust to the toppings, giving you that perfect balance of textures and flavors.

• Roasting Vegetables and Meats:

A pizza oven isn't just for pizzas. Its high temperatures make it ideal for roasting vegetables and meats as well. Place a tray of seasoned vegetables or marinated meats in the oven, and let the intense heat caramelize and enhance their natural flavors. The smoky undertones from the wood or charcoal add an extra dimension to the roasted ingredients.

• Baking Bread:

The pizza oven's high temperatures and even heat distribution make it a great tool for baking bread. Whether you're making traditional Italian bread like focaccia or experimenting with artisanal loaves, the oven's heat will help create a beautiful crust and a soft, airy interior. The wood-fired flavors will infuse the bread, adding depth to its taste.

• Enjoying Outdoor Cooking:

One of the joys of owning a pizza oven is the opportunity to cook and dine outdoors. The process of firing up the oven, tending to the fire, and watching your pizzas cook creates a memorable and enjoyable experience. It's a chance to gather with family and friends, share good food, and create lasting memories.

In conclusion, a pizza oven is a versatile tool that goes beyond just baking pizzas. Its high temperatures, even heat distribution, and wood-fired flavors enhance a wide range of dishes, from bread and roasted vegetables to grilled meats and desserts. Owning a pizza oven allows you to explore different cuisines, experiment with flavors, and enjoy the pleasures of outdoor cooking.So, fire up your pizza oven and let your culinary creativity soar!

Pizza is a beloved dish enjoyed by people all over the world. While ordering pizza from a local pizzeria is convenient, there's something special about making your own pizza from scratch. Not only is it a rewarding experience, but it also allows you to customize your pizza with your favorite toppings. If you're new to making pizza at home, there are a few pointers to keep in mind to ensure that your dough turns out perfect every time.

First and foremost, the quality of your ingredients plays a crucial role in the final outcome of your pizza. When it comes to making pizza dough, it's important to use high-quality flour. Opt for a finely ground bread flour or a type 00 flour, as they have a higher protein content, which helps create a chewy and elastic dough. Avoid using all-purpose flour, as it has a lower protein content and may result in a less desirable texture.

Another crucial ingredient in pizza dough is yeast. Yeast is responsible for the fermentation process, which gives the dough its airy and light texture. It's important to use fresh yeast or active dry yeast for the best results. If you're using active dry yeast, activate it by dissolving it in warm water with a pinch of sugar before adding it to the flour mixture. This step ensures that the yeast is active and ready to do its job.

When it comes to mixing the dough, it's important not to overwork it. Overmixing can lead to a tough and dense crust. Mix the ingredients until they come together and form a cohesive dough, then turn it out onto a lightly floured surface and knead it gently for a few minutes until it becomes smooth and elastic. The gluten in the flour needs time to develop, so allow the dough to rest for at least an hour or until it has doubled in size. This resting period allows the yeast to work its magic and gives the dough its characteristic flavor and texture.

Once the dough has risen, it's time to shape it into a pizza crust. Start by gently punching down the dough to release any air bubbles that may have formed during the rising process. Then, divide the dough into individual portions, depending on the size of the pizzas you want to make. Working with one portion at a time, shape it into a round ball and let it rest for a few minutes to relax the gluten. This step makes it easier to stretch the dough without it springing back.

When stretching the dough, be gentle and patient. Start by pressing the dough with your fingertips, gradually working your way from the center to the edges. Avoid using a rolling pin, as it can compress the dough and result in a dense crust. Instead, use your hands to stretch the dough gently, rotating it as you go to achieve an even thickness. If the dough resists stretching, let it rest for a few minutes and try again. The key is to be gentle and let gravity do most of the work.

Once you've shaped the dough, it's time to add your toppings. The possibilities are endless when it comes to pizza toppings, so feel free to get creative. However, it's important not to overload the pizza with too many toppings, as this can make it difficult to cook evenly. Start with a thin layer of tomato sauce or olive oil, then add your favorite cheeses, meats, and vegetables. Remember to season the toppings with herbs, spices, and a sprinkle of salt and pepper to enhance the flavors.

Finally, baking the pizza at the right temperature is crucial for a crispy crust and melted toppings. Preheat your oven to the highest temperature it can reach, typically around 500°F (260°C) or higher. If you have a pizza stone or a baking steel, preheat it in the oven as well. The hot surface helps cook the pizza quickly and evenly. Slide the pizza onto the preheated stone or steel using a pizza peel or a flat baking sheet. Bake the pizza for about 10-15 minutes or until the crust is golden brown and the cheese is bubbly and slightly browned.

Once the pizza is done, remove it from the oven and let it cool for a few minutes before slicing and serving. This allows the cheese to set and prevents the toppings from sliding off. Enjoy your homemade pizza with family and friends, and revel in the satisfaction of creating a delicious meal from scratch.

In conclusion, making pizza from scratch is a delightful and rewarding experience. By following these pointers, you can ensure that your pizza dough turns out perfect every time. Remember to use high-quality ingredients, allow the dough to rise and rest, be gentle when shaping the dough, and bake the pizza at a high temperature. With a little practice and experimentation, you'll be able to create your own signature pizzas that will rival those from your favorite pizzerias. So roll up your sleeves, gather your ingredients, and embark on a pizza-making adventure that will leave you craving for more.

When it comes to making pizza, having the right equipment and utensils can make a significant difference in the final result. Whether you're a professional pizzaiolo or a home cook, having the proper tools will not only make the process easier but also help you achieve that perfect pizza crust and toppings. Let's explore the essential equipment and utensils for making pizza.

• Pizza Stone or Baking Steel:

A pizza stone or baking steel is a crucial tool for achieving a crispy and evenly cooked pizza crust. These materials retain and distribute heat evenly, mimicking the effect of a traditional brick oven. Place the stone or steel in your oven and preheat it to a high temperature to create a hot surface that will crisp up the bottom of your pizza.

• Pizza Peel:

A pizza peel is a large, flat paddle used to transfer the pizza in and out of the oven. It is typically made of wood or metal and has a long handle to keep your hands away from the heat. Dust the peel with flour or cornmeal to prevent the dough from sticking, and use it to slide the pizza onto the preheated stone or steel in the oven.

• Dough Scraper:

A dough scraper is a versatile tool that comes in handy when working with pizza dough. It helps you portion the dough, scrape it off the work surface, and shape it into a ball. A stainless steel scraper is ideal as it is easy to clean and doesn't retain odors.

Stand Mixer or Mixing Bowl:

While making pizza dough can be done by hand, a stand mixer can save you time and effort. It helps knead the dough thoroughly and develops gluten, resulting in a better texture. If you don't have a stand mixer, a large mixing bowl and a sturdy wooden spoon can do the job.

• Measuring Tools:

Accurate measurements are crucial for consistent results in pizza making. Invest in a good set of measuring cups and spoons to ensure you get the right proportions of ingredients for your dough and toppings.

Rolling Pin:

A rolling pin is useful for rolling out your pizza dough into a thin, even circle. Choose a sturdy rolling pin with smooth surfaces to prevent sticking. Alternatively, you can also stretch the dough by hand, which is a traditional technique used by many pizzaiolos.

Pizza Cutter or Wheel:

Once your pizza is cooked and ready to be served, a pizza cutter or wheel is essential for slicing it into individual portions. Look for a sharp, durable cutter that can glide through the crust without dragging or tearing the toppings.

Oven Thermometer:

To ensure that your oven is reaching the desired temperature for baking pizza, an oven thermometer is handy. Ovens can vary in accuracy, and having a thermometer allows you to adjust the temperature accordingly.

Toppings and Sauce Containers:

Having an assortment of containers for your pizza toppings and sauces will help you stay organized and efficient while assembling your pizza. Small bowls or ramekins are ideal for holding ingredients like cheese, vegetables, meats, and sauces, making them easily accessible during the pizza-making process.

Pizza Cutter or Peel Stand:

A pizza cutter or peel stand is a convenient tool for storing your pizza peel and cutter when not in use. It keeps them within reach and prevents them from getting lost or damaged.

In addition to the equipment and utensils mentioned above, it's also important to have high-quality ingredients, such as fresh vegetables, meats, cheeses, and a good pizza sauce. These ingredients, combined with the right tools, will help you create delicious homemade pizzas that rival those from your favorite pizzeria.

Remember, practice makes perfect when it comes to pizza making. Experiment with different dough recipes, toppings, and cooking techniques to find your own signature pizza. With the right equipment and utensils, you'll be well-equipped to embark on your pizza-making journey and delight your family and friends with mouthwatering homemade pizzas.

Chapter 1: The Dough

Easy Pizza Dough

Prep Time: 15 Mins   Cook Time: 15 Mins   Serves: 4

Ingredients:

- 1 cup Warm Water
- 1 package Yeast (or 2 ¼ teaspoons)
- 1 teaspoon Salt
- 3 cups Flour

Directions:

1. Combine yeast and warm water. Let sit for 1 minute.
2. Add salt and flour and mix.
3. Knead until elastic or until dough pulls away from sides of bowl.
4. Let rest 15-30 minutes in a warm draft free location, usually shoot for 20 minutes.

Nutritional Value (Amount per Serving):

Calories: 474; Fat: 1.57; Carb: 86.24; Protein: 26.88

Basic Pizza Dough

Prep Time: 10 Mins   Cook Time: 10 Mins   Serves: 8

Ingredients:

- 1 ½ cup water warm
- 1 teaspoon sugar
- 2 ¼ teaspoon active dry yeast (1 package)
- 4 cups all-purpose flour
- 1 teaspoon salt
- ⅓ cup olive oil

Directions:

1. In a small bowl whisk the water, sugar and yeast together. Let it sit for about 10 minutes. If the yeast is good, it will start to froth up.
2. In the bowl of your mixer, add the flour and salt, olive oil and yeast mixture. Mix everything together using the dough hook for about 5 minutes or until the dough is soft and elastic. When it's done it will come clean from the side of the bowl.
3. Shape the dough into a ball and place in an oiled bowl, rubbing oil on the dough as well, cover with plastic wrap and refrigerate. If you're not using the dough right away, you can also freeze the dough.

Nutritional Value (Amount per Serving):

Calories: 311; Fat: 9.61; Carb: 48.47; Protein: 6.91

Pesto Pizza Dough

Prep Time: 15 Mins   Cook Time: 1 Hr 15 Mins   Serves: 4

Ingredients:

- 2 cups whole wheat flour
- 1 cup all-purpose flour
- 2 tsp active dry yeast
- 1 tsp salt
- 1 cup lukewarm water
- 2 tbsp olive oil
- 1 tbsp honey

Directions:

1. In a large mixing bowl, combine the whole wheat flour, all-purpose flour, yeast, and salt.
2. Make a well in the center of the dry ingredients and add the lukewarm water, olive oil, and honey. Stir until the dough starts to come together.
3. Transfer the dough to a floured surface and knead for about 10 minutes or until the dough becomes smooth and elastic.
4. Place the dough in a greased bowl, cover it with a clean kitchen towel, and let it rise for 1 hour or until doubled in size.

Nutritional Value (Amount per Serving):

Calories: 400; Fat: 8.71; Carb: 72.18; Protein: 11.98

Chicken Pizza Dough

Prep Time: 20 Mins   Cook Time: 1 Hr 10 Mins   Serves: 4

Ingredients:

- 2 cups whole wheat flour
- 1 cup all-purpose flour
- 2 tsp active dry yeast
- 1 tsp salt
- 1 cup lukewarm water
- 2 tbsp olive oil
- 1 tbsp honey

Directions:

1. In a large mixing bowl, combine the whole wheat flour, all-purpose flour, yeast, and salt.
2. Make a well in the center of the dry ingredients and add the lukewarm water, olive oil, and honey. Stir until the dough starts to come together.
3. Transfer the dough to a floured surface and knead for about 10 minutes or until the dough becomes smooth and elastic.
4. Place the dough in a greased bowl, cover it with a clean kitchen towel, and let it rise for 1 hour or until doubled in size.

Nutritional Value (Amount per Serving):

Calories: 400; Fat: 8.71; Carb: 72.18; Protein: 11.98

Parmesan Pizza Dough

Prep Time: 20 Mins   Cook Time: 55 Mins   Serves: 4

Ingredients:

- 2 cups whole wheat flour
- 1 cup all-purpose flour
- 2 tsp active dry yeast
- 1 tsp salt
- 1 cup lukewarm water
- 2 tbsp olive oil
- 1 tbsp honey

Directions:

1. Combine the whole wheat flour, all-purpose flour, yeast, salt, garlic powder, and grated Parmesan cheese.
2. Make a well in the center of the dry ingredients and add the lukewarm water, olive oil, and honey. Stir until the dough starts to come together.
3. Transfer the dough to a floured surface and knead for about 10 minutes or until the dough becomes smooth and elastic.
4. Place the dough in a greased bowl, cover it with a clean kitchen towel, and let it rise for 1 hour or until doubled in size.

Nutritional Value (Amount per Serving):

Calories: 400; Fat: 8.71; Carb: 72.18; Protein: 11.98

Pizza Dough Ready for Baking

Prep Time: 10 Mins   Cook Time: 50 Mins   Serves: 4

Ingredients:

- 1/2 cup lukewarm water
- 1 teaspoon active dry yeast
- 3/4 teaspoon sugar
- 3/4 teaspoon salt
- 3/4 cup all-purpose flour
- 2 tablespoons olive oil

Directions:

1. Start by combining warm water with your yeast and some sugar. It should start to froth up after a few minutes. If it doesn't, toss it and start again. You water may be too warm or your yeast may be bad. Once it's frothy, add in the vegetable oil.
2. Making pizza dough: Combine the salt and the flour, and start adding the flour to the mixer, 1/2 cup at a time.
3. Once you have added the flour, the dough will still look pretty wet and sticky. It will not pull away from the sides of the mixer by itself, but you should be able to scrape it down with a spatula.
4. Grease a large bowl. I usually just pour some vegetable oil or olive oil in the bottom of the bowl, then scrape the dough out into the bowl. You will need

a spatula to scrape the dough from the mixer bowl. Then using greased hands, turn the dough over to coat the outside of the dough in the oil.

5. Cover the dough with a towel or greased plastic wrap and allow it to rise until it is double in size. This usually takes about an hour, depending on how warm the house is.

6. Sprinkle some flour on a work surface. Lightly punch the dough down, then turn it out onto the floured surface.

Nutritional Value (Amount per Serving):

Calories: 150; Fat: 7.06; Carb: 18.78; Protein: 2.83

Neapolitan Pizza Dough (70% Hydration)

Prep Time: 15 Mins   Cook Time: 1 Hr 15 Mins   Serves: 4-6

Ingredients:

- 1 1/4 cups ripe (fed) sourdough starter
- 3/4 cup lukewarm water
- 3 1/2 cups bread flour
- 3 Tbsp olive oil
- 1 Tbsp honey
- 1 1/2 tsp salt

Directions:

1. In a large mixing bowl, combine the sourdough starter, water, and honey. Stir until the starter is dissolved. Let it sit for 5 minutes or until the mixture becomes frothy.

2. Add the flour, olive oil, and salt to the bowl. Mix everything together until a shaggy dough forms.

3. Transfer the dough onto a clean surface and knead it for about 10 minutes, until it becomes smooth and elastic. If the dough feels too dry, add a little more water. If it's too sticky, add a little more flour.

4. Place the dough in a greased bowl, cover it with a damp kitchen towel or plastic wrap, and let it rise for 1 hour in a warm place. The dough should double in size.

5. After the first rise, gently deflate the dough by folding it over a few times. Divide the dough into 4 to 6 equal portions, depending on the desired size of your pizzas.

Nutritional Value (Amount per Serving):

Calories: 156; Fat: 8.99; Carb: 17.02; Protein: 2.51

Old School Naples Dough at 70% Hydration

Prep Time: 20 Mins   Cook Time: 1 Hr 10 Mins   Serves: 4

- 1-1/4 cups lukewarm water
- 1 tsp active dry yeast
- 3 cups bread flour
- 2 Tbsp olive oil
- 1 Tbsp sugar
- 1-1/2 tsp salt

Directions:

1. In a small bowl, combine the lukewarm water, yeast, and sugar. Let it sit for 5 minutes or until frothy.
2. In a large mixing bowl, whisk together the flour and salt. Make a well in the center and pour in the yeast mixture and olive oil. Stir until the dough starts to come together.
3. Transfer the dough to a lightly floured surface and knead for about 15 minutes or until smooth and elastic. Add more flour if necessary to prevent sticking, but keep in mind that the dough should be slightly sticky.
4. Shape the dough into a ball and place it in a greased bowl. Cover with a clean kitchen towel and let it rise for 1 hour or until doubled in size.

Nutritional Value (Amount per Serving):

Calories: 141; Fat: 7.7; Carb: 15.38; Protein: 2.73

Quick Easy Pizza Dough

Prep Time: 10 Mins   Cook Time: 30 Mins   Serves: 10

Ingredients:

- 1 1/4 cups
- 110-115°F Warm Water
- 1 tsp Honey/granulated sugar
- 1/3 Olive Oil
- 1/2 tsp Active Dry Yeast
- 3 1/3 Bread Flour
- 1/2 Tbsp Salt

Directions:

1. Activate the yeast – In a large mixing bowl, stir together warm water and honey. Sprinkle with yeast and stir to combine. Let the mixture rest for 10 minutes or until it begins to foam at the top.
2. Add oil, flour, and salt to the bowl with the yeast mixture, using a wooden spoon to bring the dough together.
3. Knead – Turn the dough out and knead for 5 minutes. Sprinkle with flour if it's too sticky but keep in mind, it will start out a bit tacky but will become less so as you knead. Continue until the dough is smooth and bounces back when you gently press it with your finger.
4. Rest – Drizzle a new bowl with olive oil, then place the dough ball into the bottom of the bowl and turn to coat. Cover the bowl and leave the dough to rise on the counter for 1 ½ hours, until it's doubled in size. It's time to turn

your homemade dough into the pizza of your dreams!

Nutritional Value (Amount per Serving):

Calories: 23; Fat: 0.69; Carb: 3.62; Protein: 0.67

Whole Wheat Herb Pizza Dough

Prep Time: 15 Mins   Cook Time: 1 Hr 15 Mins   Serves: 4

Ingredients:

- 2 cups whole wheat flour
- 1 cup all-purpose flour
- 2 tsp dried Italian herbs
- 2 tsp active dry yeast
- 1 tsp salt
- 1 cup lukewarm water
- 2 tbsp olive oil
- 1 tbsp honey

Directions:

1. In a large mixing bowl, combine the whole wheat flour, all-purpose flour, dried Italian herbs, yeast, and salt.
2. Make a well in the center of the dry ingredients and add the lukewarm water, olive oil, and honey. Stir until the dough starts to come together.
3. Transfer the dough to a floured surface and knead for about 10 minutes or until the dough becomes smooth and elastic.
4. Place the dough in a greased bowl, cover it with a clean kitchen towel, and let it rise for 1 hour or until doubled in size.

Nutritional Value (Amount per Serving):

Calories: 400; Fat: 8.71; Carb: 72.18; Protein: 11.98

Classic Neapolitan Pizza Dough (60% Hydration)

Prep Time: 15 Mins   Cook Time: 1 Hr   Serves: 4-6

Ingredients:

- 1 cup ripe (fed) sourdough starter
- 1/2 cup lukewarm water
- 3 1/2 cups bread flour
- 2 Tbsp olive oil
- 1 tsp honey
- 2 tsp salt

Directions:

1. In a large mixing bowl, combine the sourdough starter, water, and honey. Stir until the starter is dissolved. Let it sit for 5 minutes or until the mixture becomes frothy.
2. Add the flour, olive oil, and salt to the bowl. Mix everything together until a shaggy dough forms.
3. Transfer the dough onto a clean surface and knead it for about 10 minutes,

until it becomes smooth and elastic. If the dough feels too dry, add a little more water. If it's too sticky, add a little more flour.

4. Place the dough in a greased bowl, cover it with a damp kitchen towel or plastic wrap, and let it rise for 1 hour in a warm place. The dough should double in size.
5. After the first rise, gently deflate the dough by folding it over a few times. Divide the dough into 4 to 6 equal portions, depending on the desired size of your pizzas.

Nutritional Value (Amount per Serving):

Calories: 123; Fat: 6.28; Carb: 14.44; Protein: 2.43

Roman Dough at 67% Hydration

Prep Time: 15 Mins   Cook Time: 1 Hr 15 Mins   Serves: 4

Ingredients:

- 1 1/4 cups lukewarm water
- 1/2 teaspoon active dry yeast
- 3 cups bread flour
- 3 tablespoons olive oil
- 1 1/2 teaspoons salt

Directions:

1. In a small bowl, dissolve the yeast in lukewarm water and let it sit for 5 minutes or until foamy.
2. In a large mixing bowl, combine the flour and salt. Make a well in the center and pour in the yeast mixture and olive oil.
3. Stir the ingredients together until a shaggy dough forms.
4. Transfer the dough to a lightly floured surface and knead for about 10 minutes until the dough becomes smooth and elastic.
5. Shape the dough into a ball and place it in a greased bowl. Cover the bowl with a clean kitchen towel and let the dough rise for 1 hour or until doubled in size.

Nutritional Value (Amount per Serving):

Calories: 161; Fat: 11.04; Carb: 13.18; Protein: 2.53

Chapter 2: Sauces and Condiments

Romesco Sauce

Prep Time: 10 Mins   Cook Time: 15 Mins   Serves: 1

Ingredients:

- 1 cup roasted red peppers, drained
- 1/2 cup almonds, toasted
- 2 cloves garlic
- 2 tbsp tomato paste
- 2 tbsp red wine vinegar
- 1 tbsp olive oil
- 1 tsp smoked paprika
- 1/2 tsp salt
- 1/4 tsp black pepper

Directions:

1. In a blender or food processor, combine the roasted red peppers, toasted almonds, garlic, tomato paste, red wine vinegar, olive oil, smoked paprika, salt, and black pepper.
2. Blend until smooth.
3. Transfer the sauce to a saucepan and heat over medium-low heat, stirring occasionally, until warmed through, about 5 minutes.
4. Remove from heat and let the sauce cool.
5. Transfer the sauce to a jar or bottle and store in the refrigerator. The flavors will develop over time.

Nutritional Value (Amount per Serving):

Calories: 210; Fat: 14.57; Carb: 18.98; Protein: 3.54

Sweet Tomato Sauce

Prep Time: 15 Mins   Cook Time: 30 Mins   Serves: 6

Ingredients:

- 2 Tbsp olive oil
- 1 onion, finely chopped
- 2 cloves garlic, minced
- 1 can (28 oz) crushed tomatoes
- 1 can (6 oz) tomato paste
- 2 Tbsp sugar
- 1 tsp dried basil
- 1 tsp dried oregano
- 1/2 tsp salt
- 1/4 tsp black pepper

Directions:

1. Heat olive oil in a large saucepan over medium heat. Add the chopped onion and minced garlic. Cook until the onion is soft and translucent.
2. Add the crushed tomatoes, tomato paste, sugar, dried basil, dried oregano, salt, and black pepper to the saucepan. Stir well to combine.
3. Bring the sauce to a simmer, then reduce the heat to low. Cover and let it cook for 20 minutes, stirring occasionally.
4. Remove the lid and continue to simmer for another 10 minutes to thicken

the sauce.

5. Taste and adjust the seasoning if needed. Serve the sweet tomato sauce over pasta or use it as a base for pizza.

Calories: 120; Fat: 5.07; Carb: 18.5; Protein: 3.09

No-cook Pizza Sauce

Prep Time: 5 Mins   Cook Time: 5 Mins   Serves: 2-3

Ingredients:

- 14.5-ounce can diced tomatoes, undrained
- 6-ounce can tomato paste
- 1 teaspoon sugar
- ½ teaspoon dried oregano
- ¼ teaspoon garlic salt
- ½ teaspoon dried basil
- Pinch of crushed red pepper

Directions:

1. Combine all ingredients in food processor or blender and blend until desired consistency.
2. Adjust seasonings and salt and pepper to taste.

Calories: 79; Fat: 0.69; Carb: 17.89; Protein: 3.87

Homemade Pizza Sauce

Prep Time: 10 Mins   Cook Time: 15 Mins   Serves: 8

Ingredients:

- 1 tablespoon olive oil
- 1 small onion or 3 shallots, grated
- 3 cloves garlic minced
- 6 ounce tomato paste 1 can
- 15 ounce tomato sauce 1 can
- 1 tablespoon Italian seasoning
- ½ teaspoon salt or to taste
- ½ teaspoon pepper or to taste
- 1½ teaspoon sugar granulated, or to taste
- 1 teaspoon red pepper flakes(Optional)

1. Heat the olive oil in a saucepan over medium-high heat. Add the grated onion and cook, stirring often, until the onion just begins to brown. 4-5 minutes.
2. Add the garlic and cook for another 30 seconds or until aromatic. Stir in the tomato paste and let it cook for 1 minute before adding the tomato sauce, Italian seasoning, salt, pepper, sugar, and red pepper flakes (if you're using them). Stir everything well to combine.
3. Let the sauce come to a bubble, then reduce the heat to low. Simmer, and stir occasionally, for 5-10 minutes, or until thickened to your preference.

Nutritional Value (Amount per Serving):

Calories: 53; Fat: 1.94; Carb: 8.44; Protein: 1.61

Basic Pizza Sauce

Prep Time: 10 Mins   Cook Time: 30 Mins   Serves: 4

Ingredients:

- 1 can (28-ounces) whole peeled tomatoes, in juice
- 1 small white or sweet onion, finely diced and minced
- 1 clove garlic, peeled and minced
- 3 to 4 fresh basil leaves
- 1 teaspoon dried oregano
- Pinch salt
- Pinch fresh ground black pepper
- Pinch sugar, optional
- 2 tablespoons olive oil, to saute

Directions:

1. Empty the contents of the tomato can in a mixing bowl and coarsely crush the tomatoes with a fork or your hands, leaving them just a little chunky.
2. In a heavy bottom 2-quart saucepot, add the olive oil, over a medium high flame and heat a little. Add the onions and saute until slightly translucent. Add the garlic and saute about a minute until golden.
3. Quickly add the crushed tomatoes to the mix. Stir well and bring to a simmer. Season with salt and pepper, to taste, and add the fresh basil and oregano.
4. Add a touch of sugar if desired or if tomatoes are tart. Simmer on a low flame, stirring often for at least 15 minutes. If not using right away, cool down and store in airtight container in the refrigerator, up to 1 week.

Nutritional Value (Amount per Serving):

Calories: 108; Fat: 6.97; Carb: 11.39; Protein: 1.34

Honey Mustard Sauce

Prep Time: 5 Mins   Cook Time: 5 Mins   Serves: 4

Ingredients:

- 1/4 cup mayonnaise
- 2 tablespoons Dijon mustard
- 2 tablespoons honey
- 1 tablespoon lemon juice
- 1/4 teaspoon garlic powder
- Salt and pepper to taste

Directions:

1. In a small bowl, whisk together mayonnaise, Dijon mustard, honey, lemon juice, garlic powder, salt, and pepper until well combined.
2. Taste and adjust the seasoning, adding more salt, pepper, or honey to suit your preference.
3. Serve immediately or refrigerate for later use. The sauce will thicken slightly when chilled.

Nutritional Value (Amount per Serving):

Calories: 91; Fat: 5.06; Carb: 11.04; Protein: 1.49

Sundried Tomato Sauce

Prep Time: 10 Mins   Cook Time: 10 Mins   Serves: 1

Ingredients:

- 1/2 cup sundried tomatoes, drained and chopped
- 2 cloves garlic, minced
- 2 tbsp olive oil
- 1/4 cup vegetable broth
- 1 tbsp tomato paste
- 1 tsp dried basil
- 1/2 tsp dried oregano
- 1/4 tsp salt
- 1/4 tsp black pepper

Directions:

1. In a small saucepan, heat the olive oil over medium heat. Add the minced garlic and cook until fragrant, about 1 minute.
2. Add the chopped sundried tomatoes, vegetable broth, tomato paste, dried basil, dried oregano, salt, and black pepper. Stir well to combine.
3. Reduce the heat to low and let the sauce simmer for 5 minutes, stirring occasionally.
4. Remove from heat and let the sauce cool.
5. Transfer the sauce to a jar or bottle and store in the refrigerator. The flavors will develop over time.

Nutritional Value (Amount per Serving):

Calories: 805; Fat: 82.48; Carb: 21.19; Protein: 5.16

Chapter 3: Charcuterie and Meat Pizzas

Pancetta Caramelized Onion Pizza

Prep Time: 10 Mins   Cook Time: 25 Mins   Serves: 4

Ingredients:

- 1 pound pizza dough
- 4 ounces pancetta, thinly sliced
- 1 large onion, thinly sliced
- 2 tablespoons olive oil
- 1 cup shredded mozzarella cheese
- 1 cup grated Parmesan cheese
- 1 cup arugula
- Salt and pepper to taste

Directions:

1. Preheat your oven to the highest temperature possible. If you have a pizza stone, place it in the oven to preheat as well.
2. In a skillet, cook the pancetta over medium heat until crispy. Remove the pancetta from the skillet and set aside.
3. In the same skillet, add the olive oil and sliced onions. Cook the onions over low heat, stirring occasionally, until they are caramelized and golden brown. This process may take about 20-30 minutes. Season with salt and pepper to taste.
4. Roll out the pizza dough on a lightly floured surface to your desired thickness.
5. Transfer the rolled-out dough to a pizza peel or baking sheet lined with parchment paper.
6. Spread the caramelized onions evenly over the dough, leaving a small border around the edges.
7. Sprinkle the shredded mozzarella cheese and grated Parmesan cheese over the onions.
8. Distribute the cooked pancetta evenly over the cheese.
9. Transfer the pizza to the preheated oven and bake for a few minutes, or until the crust is golden brown and the cheese is melted and bubbly.
10. Remove the pizza from the oven and let it cool for a few minutes. Top with fresh arugula before serving.

Nutritional Value (Amount per Serving):

Calories: 649; Fat: 38.69; Carb: 41.55; Protein: 34.22

Classic Pepperoni Pizza

Prep Time: 15 Mins   Cook Time: 15-20 Mins   Serves: 4

Ingredients:

- 1 pizza dough
- ½ cup pizza sauce

- 1 ½ cups shredded mozzarella cheese
- ¼ cup sliced pepperoni
- ½ cup roasted red bell pepper strips
- 1 tablespoon olive oil
- 1 teaspoon dried oregano
- Salt and pepper to taste

Directions:

1. Preheat the oven to the temperature specified on the pizza dough package or if using homemade dough.
2. Roll out the pizza dough on a floured surface to your desired thickness.
3. Transfer the rolled-out dough to a pizza stone or a baking sheet lined with parchment paper.
4. Spread the pizza sauce evenly over the dough, leaving a small border around the edges.
5. Sprinkle the shredded mozzarella cheese over the sauce, covering the entire surface.
6. Arrange the pepperoni slices and roasted red bell pepper strips on top of the cheese.
7. Drizzle the olive oil over the pizza and sprinkle with dried oregano, salt, and pepper.
8. Place the pizza in the preheated oven and bake for 15-20 minutes, or until the crust is golden brown and the cheese is bubbly and slightly browned.
9. Remove the pizza from the oven and let it cool for a few minutes before slicing and serving. Enjoy!

Nutritional Value (Amount per Serving):

Calories: 501; Fat: 16.9; Carb: 54.93; Protein: 32.91

Meat-Za Pie

Prep Time: 20 Mins   Cook Time: 4 Mins   Serves: 4

Ingredients:

- 1 can (5 ounces) evaporated milk
- 1/2 cup plain or seasoned dry bread crumbs
- 3/4 teaspoon garlic salt
- 1 pound lean ground beef
- 1/4 cup ketchup
- 1 teaspoon sugar
- 1/2 cup canned sliced mushrooms
- 1/4 teaspoon dried oregano
- 2 tablespoons grated Parmesan cheese

- 3 slices process American cheese, cut into thin strips

Directions:

1. In a large bowl, combine the milk, bread crumbs and garlic salt; add beef. Stir with a fork just until mixed. Press onto the bottom and 1/2 in. up the sides of an ungreased 9-in. pie plate.
2. Combine ketchup and sugar; spread over beef mixture. Sprinkle with mushrooms. Sprinkle with oregano and Parmesan cheese.
3. Bake for 20 minutes or until meat is no longer pink; drain. Arrange American cheese in a lattice pattern on top. Cut into wedges.

Nutritional Value (Amount per Serving):

Calories: 404; Fat: 19.67; Carb: 17.61; Protein: 37.33

Magical Meat Feast Pizza

Prep Time: 5 Mins   Cook Time: 15 Mins   Serves: 1

Ingredients:

- 1 piece of Lo-Dough
- 0.04lb ham
- 0.04lb cooked chicken breast
- 0.05lb lean spicy mince, cooked
- 0.03lb pepperoni
- 0.22lb mozzarella
- 2 tsp of passata
- A twist of black pepper

Directions:

1. Preheat your oven.
2. Spread the passata across the Lo-Dough in a thin layer, right up to the edge.
3. Spread the grated cheese on top of the passata and add the ham, chicken, beef and pepperoni. 4. Put the pizza in the oven for 7 minutes or until golden and bubbling.
4. Serve with a crack of black pepper on top.

Nutritional Value (Amount per Serving):

Calories: 437; Fat: 12.87; Carb: 30.29; Protein: 49.82

Chorizo Pizza with Goat Cheese

Prep Time: 15 Mins   Cook Time: 20 Mins   Serves: 4

Ingredients:

- 1 pre-made pizza dough
- 1/2 cup tomato sauce
- 4 ounces chorizo, sliced
- 2 cups sautéed greens (such as spinach, kale, or Swiss chard)
- 4 ounces goat cheese, crumbled

- 1/4 cup sliced red onions
- 1/4 cup sliced black olives
- 1/4 teaspoon red pepper flakes

(optional)
- Salt and pepper to taste

Directions:

1. Preheat the oven to the temperature specified on the pizza dough package.
2. Roll out the pizza dough on a floured surface to your desired thickness.
3. Transfer the rolled-out dough to a pizza stone or baking sheet.
4. Spread the tomato sauce evenly over the dough, leaving a small border around the edges.
5. Arrange the sliced chorizo, sautéed greens, crumbled goat cheese, sliced red onions, and black olives on top of the sauce.
6. Season with salt, pepper, and red pepper flakes if desired.
7. Bake the pizza in the preheated oven according to the instructions on the pizza dough package, or until the crust is golden brown and the cheese is melted and bubbly.
8. Remove the pizza from the oven and let it cool slightly before slicing and serving.

Nutritional Value (Amount per Serving):

Calories: 427; Fat: 24.09; Carb: 33.98; Protein: 19

3. Meat Pizza Casserole

Prep Time: 20 Mins   Cook Time: 1 Hour 5 Mins   Serves: 8

Ingredients:

- 1 lb bow tie pasta
- 1/2-1 lb mild pork sausage
- 1 large onion, medium size chopped
- 2 (26 ounce) jars spaghetti sauce (I used Bertolli's Mushroom and Garlic)
- 1/2-1 lb cubed cooked ham
- 1/2-1 lb of sliced pepperoni
- 3 (8 ounce) bags of shredded mozzarella cheese
- 6 tablespoons of grated parmesan cheese
- 2 tablespoons chopped garlic
- 1 teaspoon dried oregano

Directions:

1. Cook pasta in boiling water until all denté.
2. Cook sausage, garlic powder and oregano with onions until the juices run clear.
3. In a lightly greased 9x13x3 inch pan, pour a small amount of sauce to lightly coat bottom.

4. Layer ingredients in the order listed below.

5. 1st layer-1/3 of the pasta, 1/3 remaining sauce, 1 bag of mozzarella cheese, 2 Tablespoons parmesan cheese, sausage and onions.

6. 2nd layer-1/2 of the remaining pasta, 1/2 remaining sauce, 1 bag of mozzarella cheese, 2 Tablespoons parmesan cheese, ham.

7. 3rd layer-all remaining pasta, all remaining sauce, 1 bag of mozzarella cheese, 2 Tablespoons parmesan cheese, all the pepperoni (completely covering the entire top with pepperoni).

8. Bake for 40 minutes.

9. Let sit for 5 minutes before serving.

Nutritional Value (Amount per Serving):

Calories: 537; Fat: 30.43; Carb: 26.42; Protein: 38.61

Pancetta Pizza with Balsamic Glaze

Prep Time: 20 Mins   Cook Time: 20 Mins   Serves: 4

Ingredients:

- 1 pound pizza dough
- 4 ounces pancetta, thinly sliced
- 1 large onion, thinly sliced
- 2 tablespoons olive oil
- 1 cup shredded mozzarella cheese
- 1 cup grated Parmesan cheese
- Balsamic glaze (store-bought or homemade)
- Fresh basil leaves for garnish
- Salt and pepper to taste

Directions:

1. Preheat your oven. If you have a pizza stone, place it in the oven to preheat as well.

2. In a skillet, cook the pancetta over medium heat until crispy. Remove the pancetta from the skillet and set aside.

3. In the same skillet, add the olive oil and sliced onions. Cook the onions over low heat, stirring occasionally, until they are caramelized and golden brown. This process may take about 20-30 minutes. Season with salt and pepper to taste.

4. Roll out the pizza dough on a lightly floured surface to your desired thickness.

5. Transfer the rolled-out dough to a pizza peel or baking sheet lined with parchment paper.

6. Spread the caramelized onions evenly over the dough, leaving a small border around the edges.

7. Sprinkle the shredded mozzarella cheese and grated Parmesan cheese over the onions.

8. Distribute the cooked pancetta evenly over the cheese.

9. Transfer the pizza to the preheated oven and bake for about 10-12 minutes, or until the crust is golden brown and the cheese is melted and bubbly.
10. Remove the pizza from the oven and drizzle balsamic glaze over the top. Garnish with fresh basil leaves before serving.

Nutritional Value (Amount per Serving):

Calories: 653; Fat: 38.71; Carb: 42.51; Protein: 34.4

Red Braised Pork Belly Pizza

Prep Time: 1 Hour   Cook Time: 1 Hr 45 Mins   Serves: 8

Ingredients:

- 1 Wild Dough
- 1½ cups Red Braised Pork Belly instructions below
- 1 cup Bok Choy
- ½ cup Red Pepper
- ⅓ cup Red Onion
- 2 cups Mozzarella Cheese
- 1 cup Sweet Chili Sauce
- Red Braised Pork Belly
- 1 lb Pork Belly
- Water for boiling
- 2 tbsp Ginger
- 4 Green Onions
- 1 Serrano Chili
- 1 cup Water hot
- ¼ cup Brown Sugar
- ¼ cup Soy Sauce
- 1 tbsp Rice Wine Vinegar
- 1 tbsp Ginger ground
- 1 tsp Chinese Five Spice ground

Directions:

1. Peel and slice ginger, chop green onions, slice serrano chili lengthwise, pork belly into cubes.
2. In large wok, fill half way with water and bring to a boil. Add ginger, onions, serrano chili and pork belly. Bring to a boil, reduce heat and cook for 5 minutes. Remove pork belly from wok, discard water, ginger, onion and chili.
3. Heat wok to med-high heat and add oil. Add pork belly and cook until golden brown, then remove pork belly from wok.
4. Add brown sugar to wok and melt slightly (careful not to burn sugar). Add hot water and mix well. Add soy sauce, rice wine vinegar, Chinese five spice, and ground ginger. Add pork belly and stir well to coat the pork belly in the sauce. Cover and cook on low for 30 minutes.
5. Remove lid and cook for 10 minutes. Remove pork belly and cut into ⅛ inch slices when cool.
6. Preheat oven with baking steel or pizza stone inside the oven for 1 hour.
7. Flour surface and roll out the dough. Put a floured pizza peel underneath the dough. Add sauce, cheese, and toppings. Pat down the toppings before putting into the oven. Bake pizza in the oven for 8-10 minutes. Remove

pizza from oven and let cool for 5 minutes.

Calories: 419; Fat: 14.32; Carb: 36.69; Protein: 35.84

Italian Easter Meat Pie-Pizza Gaina

Prep Time: 20 Mins   Cook Time: 45 Mins   Serves: 8

Ingredients:

- or The Crust
- 3 cups all-purpose flour plus more for dusting
- ¾ teaspoon baking powder
- ½ teaspoon salt
- 8 tablespoons unsalted butter cut into cubes, chilled
- 2 large eggs
- ½ cup ice water
- illing
- 1½ pounds ricotta
- 3 large eggs
- 8 ounces packaged mozzarella cut into 1/2-inch dice
- 4 ounces Genoa salami cut into 1/2-inch dice
- 4 ounces mortadella cut into 1/2-inch dice
- 4 ounces prosciutto crudo cut into 1/2-inch dice
- 4 ounces ham cut into 1/2-inch dice
- 2 Tablespoons grated parmigiano-Reggiano
- 2 Tablespoons grated pecorino
- 2 tablespoons parsley chopped, optional
- FOR THE EGG WASH
- 1 large egg yolk mixed with 1 tablespoon water

Directions:

1. Prep the dough: In the bowl of food processor, add the flour, baking powder and salt. Give it a pulse to combine. Add the cold cubed butter. Pulse until the mixture is like a coarse meal (should be pea sized pieces of dough).
2. Pulse the processor: Pulse until the mixture is like a coarse meal (should be pea sized pieces of dough).
3. Add in eggs: Add the eggs and water. Pulse until a couple times to combine.
4. Knead the dough: Remove the dough onto a clean counter or work surface. Knead it to bring it together (we aren't overworking dough. Just bringing it together by kneading a little bit).
5. Portion out the dough: Divide the dough into two portions (one portions is 1/3 of dough and the other is 2/3).

6. Rest the dough: Wrap with plastic wrap and let it rest for 20 minutes.
7. Bake the savory pie: Preheat oven to 375F.
8. Butter and flour a 9-inch spring form pan.
9. On a clean work surface, roll out the larger portion of the dough to 15-inch round.
10. Carefully place into the bottom of spring form pan.
11. Place in the refrigerator while you prep the filling. Place the other wrapped portion of dough also in the fridge .
12. Prep the filling: In a large bowl, add the ricotta and eggs.
13. Add in the all the meats and cheeses.
14. Stir everything to combine.
15. Remove the spring form pan with the crust from the refrigerator.
16. Add into bottom of pie crust: Spoon the mixture cheese/meat filling into the pie crust. Flatten it out with a spatula.
17. Cut out strips of dough: On a clean surface, roll out the remaining dough. You could cut out strips of dough or roll it to a 10-inch round. If you're using strips, place them carefully in an overlapping patter on top of the filling. If you're using one round piece, carefully transfer on top of the filling.
18. Press the edges of the pastry together.
19. Trim the edges: If you have any overhanging dough, trim the edges and tuck underneath.
20. Crimp all around the edge of the crust with a fork. Brush on the egg wash mixture. If you're using one large piece of dough on top, cut a small steam vent.
21. Bake the savory pie: Bake for 65-75 minutes, or until crust is golden (I place my pan on top of a baking sheet in case any of the cheese mixture bubbles over). Halfway through baking cover loosely with foil paper so it won't over brown.
22. Cool down the pie: Transfer pan to a baking rack. Let completely cool before removing from springform pan.
23. Slice and serve: Slice into wedges and serve. You could also refrigerate for a couple hours before slicing and serving.

Nutritional Value (Amount per Serving):

Calories: 777; Fat: 43.59; Carb: 60; Protein: 35.75

Ground Beef Pizza with Pesto

Prep Time: 20 Mins   Cook Time: 15 Mins   Serves: 4

Ingredients:

- 1 pound ground beef

- 1 pizza dough (store-bought or homemade)
- 1/2 cup basil pesto
- 1 cup shredded Asiago cheese
- 1/2 cup sliced green olives
- 1/4 cup diced red onion
- Salt and pepper to taste

Directions:

1. Preheat your oven.
2. In a skillet, cook the ground beef over medium heat until browned. Drain any excess fat.
3. Roll out the pizza dough on a floured surface to your desired thickness.
4. Transfer the dough to a greased baking sheet or pizza stone.
5. Spread the basil pesto evenly over the dough, leaving a small border around the edges.
6. Sprinkle the cooked ground beef over the pesto.
7. Top with shredded Asiago cheese, sliced green olives, and diced red onion.
8. Season with salt and pepper to taste.
9. Bake in the preheated oven for about 12-15 minutes or until the crust is golden brown and the cheese is melted and bubbly.
10. Remove from the oven, let it cool for a few minutes, then slice and serve.

Nutritional Value (Amount per Serving):

Calories: 691; Fat: 38.95; Carb: 32.56; Protein: 50.66

Ground Beef, Green Olive Asiago Pizza

Prep Time: 10 Mins   Cook Time: 25 Mins   Serves: 4

Ingredients:

- 1 pound ground beef
- 1 pizza dough (store-bought or homemade)
- 1 cup tomato sauce
- 1 cup shredded Asiago cheese
- 1/2 cup sliced green olives
- 1/2 teaspoon dried oregano
- 1/2 teaspoon garlic powder
- Salt and pepper to taste

Directions:

1. Preheat your oven.
2. In a skillet, cook the ground beef over medium heat until browned. Drain any excess fat.
3. Roll out the pizza dough on a floured surface to your desired thickness.
4. Transfer the dough to a greased baking sheet or pizza stone.
5. Spread the tomato sauce evenly over the dough, leaving a small border around the edges.

6. Sprinkle the cooked ground beef over the sauce.
7. Top with shredded Asiago cheese and sliced green olives.
8. Sprinkle dried oregano and garlic powder over the toppings. Season with salt and pepper to taste.
9. Bake in the preheated oven for about 12-15 minutes or until the crust is golden brown and the cheese is melted and bubbly.
10. Remove from the oven, let it cool for a few minutes, then slice and serve.

Nutritional Value (Amount per Serving):

Calories: 760; Fat: 39.13; Carb: 45.69; Protein: 52.27

Classic Fully-Loaded Deep-Dish Meat Pizza

Prep Time: 30 Mins   Cook Time: 35 Mins   Serves: 6-8

Ingredients:

- or The Dough:
- 3 cups all-purpose flour
- 2 teaspoons instant yeast
- 1 teaspoon sugar
- 1 teaspoon salt
- 1 cup warm water
- 2 tablespoons olive oil
- or The Pizza
- 1 pound ground beef
- 1/2 pound Italian sausage, casings removed
- 1 cup pizza sauce
- 2 cups shredded mozzarella cheese
- 1 cup sliced pepperoni
- 1/2 cup sliced black olives
- 1/2 cup sliced green bell peppers
- 1/2 cup sliced red onions
- 1/4 cup grated Parmesan cheese
- 1 teaspoon dried oregano
- 1/2 teaspoon garlic powder
- Salt and pepper to taste

Directions:

1. In a large bowl, combine the flour, yeast, sugar, and salt. Add the warm water and olive oil, and mix until a dough forms. Knead the dough on a lightly floured surface for about 5 minutes until smooth and elastic. Place the dough in a greased bowl, cover with a clean kitchen towel, and let it rise in a warm place for about 1 hour or until doubled in size.
2. Preheat your oven. Grease a deep-dish pizza pan or a cast-iron skillet. In a skillet, cook the ground beef and Italian sausage over medium heat until browned. Drain any excess fat.
3. Roll out the risen dough on a floured surface to fit the greased pizza pan. Press the dough into the pan, covering the bottom and sides. Spread the pizza sauce evenly over the dough.
4. Add the cooked ground beef and Italian sausage on top of the cheese. Sprinkle with the remaining mozzarella cheese.
5. Sprinkle the grated Parmesan cheese, dried oregano, garlic powder, salt,

and pepper over the toppings.

Nutritional Value (Amount per Serving):

Calories: 556; Fat: 20.07; Carb: 52.06; Protein: 41.71

Mega-Meat Pizza

Prep Time: 25 Mins   Cook Time: 40 Mins   Serves: 8

Ingredients:

- 1 can (11 oz) refrigerated Thin Crust Pizza Crust
- 1/2 lb lean (at least 80%) ground beef
- 1/2 lb bulk Italian sausage
- 1/2 cup pizza sauce
- 1/2 cup sliced pepperoni
- 1 oz thinly sliced deli salami, cut into quarters
- 1/2 cup diced Canadian bacon
- 1 cup shredded Cheddar cheese (4 oz)
- 1 cup shredded mozzarella cheese (4 oz)

Directions:

1. Heat oven. Spray or grease a dark or nonstick cookie sheet. Unroll dough on cookie sheet; starting at center, press out dough into a rectangle.
2. Innonstick skillet, cook beef and sausage over medium-high heat 6 to 8 minutes, stirring frequently, until beef is thoroughly cooked and sausage is no longer pink; drain.
3. Spread pizza sauce to within 1/2 inch of edges of dough. Top with cooked drained meat and remaining ingredients.
4. Bake 13 to 16 minutes or until crust is golden brown and cheese is melted.

Nutritional Value (Amount per Serving):

Calories: 374; Fat: 23.12; Carb: 12.67; Protein: 28.5

Meat Lover's Pizza Rice Skillet

Prep Time: 10 Mins   Cook Time: 20 Mins   Serves: 6

Ingredients:

- 1 pound bulk Italian sausage
- 1 can (14-1/2 ounces) diced tomatoes with basil, oregano and garlic
- 1 can (15-1/2 ounces) cannellini beans, rinsed and drained
- 1-1/2 cups water
- 1-1/2 cups uncooked instant rice

- 1/4 cup grated Parmesan cheese
- 1/2 cup (2 ounces) sliced mini pepperoni
- Optional: Additional grated Parmesan cheese and chopped fresh basil

Directions:

1. In a large skillet, cook sausage over medium heat 5-7 minutes or until no longer pink, breaking into crumbles; drain. Return to skillet with next 4 ingredients. Bring to a boil; cover and remove from heat. Let stand 5 minutes.
2. Fluff with a fork; stir in cheese. Top with pepperoni and, if desired, additional Parmesan cheese and basil.

Nutritional Value (Amount per Serving):

Calories: 352; Fat: 25.21; Carb: 16.59; Protein: 14.49

Gourmet Bocconcini Pizza with Arugula

Prep Time: 20 Mins   Cook Time: 15 Mins   Serves: 4

Ingredients:

- 1 pre-made pizza dough
- 1/2 cup marinara sauce
- 8 ounces bocconcini cheese, drained and sliced
- 4 slices prosciutto, torn into pieces
- 2 cups fresh arugula
- 1/4 cup shaved Parmesan cheese
- 1 tablespoon lemon juice
- 1 tablespoon extra-virgin olive oil
- Salt and pepper to taste

Directions:

1. Preheat your oven if using homemade dough.
2. Roll out the pizza dough on a lightly floured surface to your desired thickness.
3. Transfer the rolled-out dough to a pizza stone or baking sheet lined with parchment paper.
4. Spread the marinara sauce evenly over the dough, leaving a small border around the edges.
5. Arrange the sliced bocconcini cheese evenly over the sauce.
6. Place the torn prosciutto pieces on top of the cheese.
7. Place the pizza in the preheated oven and bake for about 15-18 minutes or until the crust is golden brown and the cheese is melted and bubbly.
8. Remove the pizza from the oven and let it cool for a few minutes.
9. In a large bowl, combine the fresh arugula, shaved Parmesan cheese, lemon juice, and extra-virgin olive oil. Toss to coat the arugula evenly.

10. Season with salt and pepper to taste.
11. Top the baked pizza with the dressed arugula.
12. Slice and serve.

Nutritional Value (Amount per Serving):

Calories: 314; Fat: 18.98; Carb: 20.46; Protein: 16.33

Prosciutto Paradise Pizza

Prep Time: 20 Mins   Cook Time: 10 Mins   Serves: 4

Ingredients:

- 1 recipe homemade pizza dough
- 2 TB olive oil
- 1 cup garlic cream sauce
- 2 cups shredded mozzarella cheese
- 4 oz. sliced prosciutto
- 1 cup arugula
- 1/4 cup shaved Parmesan cheese
- 2 tsp balsamic glaze, for garnish (optional)

Directions:

1. Preheat the oven and oil a sheet pan.
2. Shape your dough into a circle, place it on the sheet pan, then brush the top with olive oil, leaving about 1 around the edges for the crust. You can either roll the edges to create a thicker crust or leave as is. Set aside to rise for 10 minutes.
3. Spread the garlic cream sauce evenly over the dough, then top with mozzarella cheese and prosciutto.
4. Bake for 10-12 minutes or until the crust is golden brown and the cheese is melted and bubbly.
5. Remove from the oven and top with arugula and shaved Parmesan cheese.
6. Drizzle with balsamic glaze (optional), cut into slices, and serve hot.

Nutritional Value (Amount per Serving):

Calories: 340; Fat: 16.29; Carb: 20.13; Protein: 29.21

Sweet and Sour Pork Pizza

Prep Time: 1 Hr   Cook Time: 10 Mins   Serves: 8

Ingredients:

- oppings
- 2 cups Sweet and sour pork
- 2 cups Mozzarella cheese
- 1 cup Sweet and sour sauce
- weet And Sour Pork
- ½ lb Pork butt

- 1 cup Cooking oil
- 1 Egg white
- 1 Green onion
- ½ stalk Celery
- ¼ Red pepper
- ¼ Green pepper
- ¼ White onion
- ½ tsp Soy sauce
- ¼ tsp Sugar
- ¼ cup Cornstarch
- 1 cup Pineapple tidbits with juice
- 1 tbsp Cornstarch
- ¾ cup Water
- 2 tbsp Sugar
- 2 tbsp Ketchup
- 2 tbsp Apple cider vinegar
- ½ tsp Soy sauce

Directions:

1. Grate mozzarella.
2. Preheat oven with baking steel or pizza stone inside the oven for 1 hour.
3. Flour surface and roll out the dough. Put a floured pizza peel underneath the dough. Add sauce, mozzarella, and sweet and sour pork. Pat down the toppings before putting into the oven.
4. Bake pizza in the oven at 550 degrees F. for 8-10 minutes. Let cool 5 minutes then slice it up!

Nutritional Value (Amount per Serving):

Calories: 591; Fat: 37.57; Carb: 40.06; Protein: 23.93

Gorgonzola Prosciutto Pizza with Caramelized Onions

Prep Time: 20 Mins   Cook Time: 15 Mins   Serves: 4

Ingredients:

- 1 pizza dough (store-bought or homemade)
- 1/2 cup fig jam
- 1 cup crumbled Gorgonzola cheese
- 4-6 slices of prosciutto
- 1 large onion, thinly sliced
- 2 tablespoons butter
- 1 tablespoon olive oil
- Salt and pepper to taste

Directions:

1. Preheat your oven to the temperature recommended for your pizza dough.
2. In a skillet, melt the butter and olive oil over medium heat. Add the sliced onions and cook, stirring occasionally, until caramelized and golden brown, about 20-25 minutes. Season with salt and pepper to taste.
3. Roll out the pizza dough on a lightly floured surface to your desired thickness.
4. Transfer the dough to a baking sheet or pizza stone. Spread the fig jam evenly over the dough, leaving a small border around the edges.
5. Sprinkle the crumbled Gorgonzola cheese over the fig jam.
6. Tear the prosciutto into smaller pieces and distribute them over the cheese.

7. Spread the caramelized onions over the top of the pizza.
8. Bake the pizza in the preheated oven until the crust is golden and crispy, and the cheese has melted and started to brown, usually around 12-15 minutes.
9. Remove the pizza from the oven and let it cool slightly. Slice and serve while still warm. Enjoy!

Nutritional Value (Amount per Serving):

Calories: 620; Fat: 37.57; Carb: 47.97; Protein: 24.5

Chorizo Sautéed Greens Pizza with Garlic Butter

Prep Time: 20 Mins   Cook Time: 10-20 Mins   Serves: 4

Ingredients:

- 1 pizza dough (store-bought or homemade)
- 2 tablespoons butter
- 2 cloves garlic, minced
- 1/2 cup tomato sauce
- 1 cup shredded mozzarella cheese
- 1/2 cup cooked chorizo, crumbled
- 2 cups sautéed greens (such as spinach or kale)
- 1/4 cup sliced red onion
- Salt and pepper to taste

Directions:

1. Preheat your oven.
2. In a small saucepan, melt the butter over medium heat. Add the minced garlic and cook for 1-2 minutes until fragrant. Remove from heat.
3. Roll out the pizza dough on a floured surface to your desired thickness.
4. Transfer the dough to a greased baking sheet or pizza stone.
5. Brush the garlic butter mixture evenly over the dough, including the edges.
6. Spread the tomato sauce evenly over the dough, leaving a small border around the edges.
7. Sprinkle the shredded mozzarella cheese over the sauce.
8. Top with crumbled chorizo, sautéed greens, and sliced red onion.
9. Season with salt and pepper to taste.
10. Bake in the preheated oven for about 12-15 minutes or until the crust is golden brown and the cheese is melted and bubbly.
11. Remove from the oven, let it cool for a few minutes, then slice and serve.

Nutritional Value (Amount per Serving):

Calories: 491; Fat: 25.06; Carb: 41.45; Protein: 24.45

Spicy Deep-Dish Meat Pizza

Prep Time: 40 Mins   Cook Time: 40 Mins   Serves: 6-8

- or The Pizza
- 1 pound ground beef
- 1/2 pound spicy Italian sausage, casings removed
- 1 cup pizza sauce
- 2 cups shredded mozzarella cheese
- 1 cup sliced pepperoni
- 1/2 cup sliced jalapenos
- 1/2 cup sliced red onions
- 1/4 cup sliced black olives
- 1/4 cup sliced green olives
- 1 teaspoon dried oregano
- 1/2 teaspoon garlic powder
- Salt and pepper to taste

Directions:

1. In a skillet, cook the ground beef and spicy Italian sausage over medium heat until browned. Drain any excess fat.
2. Roll out the risen dough on a floured surface to fit the greased pizza pan. Press the dough into the pan, covering the bottom and sides.
3. Spread the pizza sauce evenly over the dough. Top with half of the shredded mozzarella cheese.
4. Add the cooked ground beef and spicy Italian sausage on top of the cheese. Sprinkle with the remaining mozzarella cheese.
5. Arrange the pepperoni slices, jalapenos, red onions, black olives, and green olives over the cheese.
6. Sprinkle the dried oregano, garlic powder, salt, and pepper over the toppings.
7. Bake the pizza in the preheated oven for about 30-35 minutes or until the crust is golden brown and the cheese is melted and bubbly.
8. Remove from the oven and let it cool for a few minutes before slicing and serving.

Nutritional Value (Amount per Serving):

Calories: 332; Fat: 18.46; Carb: 6.82; Protein: 33.32

Fennel Sausage Fresh Tomato Pizza

Prep Time: 30 Mins   Cook Time: 20 Mins   Serves: 4

Ingredients:

- 1 pound pizza dough
- 1/2 cup tomato sauce
- 1 cup fennel sausage, cooked and sliced
- 1 cup ricotta cheese
- 2 cups fresh tomatoes, diced
- 1 cup shredded mozzarella cheese
- 1/4 cup grated Parmesan cheese
- Fresh basil leaves, for garnish
- Olive oil
- Salt and pepper to taste

Directions:

1. Preheat your oven for your pizza dough.

2. Roll out the pizza dough on a lightly floured surface to your desired thickness.
3. Brush the dough with olive oil, covering the entire surface.
4. Spread the tomato sauce evenly over the dough, leaving a small border around the edges.
5. Arrange the sliced fennel sausage over the sauce.
6. Drop spoonfuls of ricotta cheese onto the pizza, distributing it evenly.
7. Sprinkle the diced fresh tomatoes over the toppings.
8. Sprinkle the shredded mozzarella cheese and grated Parmesan cheese over the pizza.
9. Season with salt and pepper to taste.
10. Transfer the pizza onto a baking sheet or a preheated pizza stone.
11. Bake in the preheated oven for about 25-30 minutes or until the crust is golden and the cheese is melted and bubbly.
12. Remove from the oven and let it cool for a few minutes. Garnish with fresh basil leaves.
13. Slice and serve your delicious Fennel Sausage & Fresh Tomato Pizza.

Nutritional Value (Amount per Serving):

Calories: 600; Fat: 30.72; Carb: 48.38; Protein: 32.43

Spicy Meat Lovers Garlic Pizza

Prep Time: 15 Mins   Cook Time: 15 Mins   Serves: 2

Ingredients:

- 1 Cauliflower Pizza Crust
- 1 Clove Garlic thinly chopped (check notes)
- 1 Small Red Onion thinly sliced
- 3 Tbsp Pizza Sauce store-bought or homemade as per choice
- 3 Tbsp Cheese use any as per choice
- 1/4 Tsp Italian Seasoning
- 1/4 Tsp Chili Flakes optional
- 1-2 Fresh Basil Leaves for garnish (optional)
- Meat Toppings: (you can add or remove any as per choice)
- 2 Tbsp Pepperoni
- 1 Tbsp Chorizo use any kind you like
- 1 Italian Meatballs crumbled & cooked
- 1 Chicken Sausage small thinly sliced

Directions:

1. Cook the Cauliflower Pizza Crust (frozen)
2. Preheat oven. Place Cauliflower Pizza Crust on baking sheet and bake 16 minutes or until crisp.
3. Remove from oven and cool a little.

4. Add the Toppings and Create the Spicy Meat Lovers Garlic Pizza
5. Place the baked Cauliflower Pizza Crust on a baking tray (pizza pan if using).
6. Spread the pizza sauce evenly all over the crust (leaving the edges).
7. Sprinkle cheese on top of the crust.
8. Add chorizo, sliced chicken sausage, crumbled Italian meatballs and pepperoni.
9. Add sliced onions, garlic, Italian seasoning.
10. Sprinkle some more cheese and bake in the oven for 15 minutes.
11. After 15 minutes, remove the pizza from oven and slice into 5-6 slices.
12. Add some crushed basil leaves on top and Serve Hot

Nutritional Value (Amount per Serving):

Calories: 934; Fat: 54.77; Carb: 66.9; Protein: 42.91

Beef-Mushroom Pizza

Prep Time: 20 Mins   Cook Time: 10 Mins   Serves: 4

Ingredients:

- 1 (12 inch) whole-wheat Italian bread shell
- Reserved no-salt-added tomato paste from Wine-Braised Beef Brisket (see associated recipe)
- Reserved beef and cooking juices from Wine-Braised Beef Brisket (see associated recipe)
- 1 cup sliced fresh mushrooms
- ½ cup chopped green sweet pepper
- ¾ cup shredded reduced-fat mozzarella cheese (3 ounces)

Directions:

1. Preheat oven. Place bread shell on a large pizza pan or baking sheet lined with parchment paper; set aside. In a small bowl, whisk together tomato paste and the reserved cooking juices from the Wine-Braised Beef Brisket. Chop the reserved beef.
2. Spread tomato paste mixture over bread shell. Top with beef, mushrooms, sweet pepper and cheeses. Bake 12 to 15 minutes or until heated through and cheese is melted. Cut into 6 wedges to serve.

Nutritional Value (Amount per Serving):

Calories: 721; Fat: 28.28; Carb: 11.06; Protein: 106.68

Chapter 4: Vegetable Pizzas

Shaved Asparagus Herb Pizza with Egg

Prep Time: 5 Mins   Cook Time: 20 Mins   Serves: 4

Ingredients:

- 1 pizza dough
- 1 bunch asparagus
- 2 tablespoons olive oil
- Salt and pepper to taste
- 1 cup shredded mozzarella cheese
- 2 tablespoons chopped fresh herbs (such as basil, parsley, or chives)
- 4 large eggs

Directions:

1. Preheat your oven to the highest temperature.
2. Roll out the pizza dough into a thin circle on a floured surface.
3. Trim the tough ends of the asparagus and use a vegetable peeler to shave thin ribbons.
4. In a bowl, toss the asparagus ribbons with olive oil, salt, and pepper.
5. Spread the shredded mozzarella cheese evenly over the pizza dough.
6. Arrange the shaved asparagus on top of the cheese.
7. Sprinkle the chopped fresh herbs over the asparagus.
8. Carefully crack the eggs onto the pizza, spacing them evenly.
9. Transfer the pizza to a baking sheet or pizza stone and bake for about 10-12 minutes, or until the crust is golden and the eggs are cooked to your liking.
10. Remove from the oven and let it cool slightly before slicing and serving.

Nutritional Value (Amount per Serving):

Calories: 549; Fat: 24.36; Carb: 52.59; Protein: 30.38

Wild Mushroom, Kale Fontina Pizza

Prep Time: 15 Mins   Cook Time: 15 Mins   Serves: 2

Ingredients:

- 1 pizza dough
- 1 cup sliced wild mushrooms (such as shiitake, oyster, or cremini)
- 2 cups chopped kale leaves
- 2 tablespoons olive oil
- 2 cloves garlic, minced
- Salt and pepper to taste
- 1 cup shredded fontina cheese
- 1/4 cup grated Parmesan cheese

Directions:

1. Preheat your oven to the highest temperature.
2. Roll out the pizza dough into a thin circle on a floured surface.
3. In a skillet, heat the olive oil over medium heat. Add the minced garlic and sauté for about 1 minute until fragrant.
4. Add the sliced mushrooms to the skillet and cook until they release their moisture and become tender, about 5-7 minutes.
5. Add the chopped kale to the skillet and cook until wilted, about 2-3 minutes.
6. Season the mushroom and kale mixture with salt and pepper to taste.
7. Spread the shredded fontina cheese evenly over the pizza dough.
8. Spoon the mushroom and kale mixture over the cheese.
9. Sprinkle the grated Parmesan cheese over the top.
10. Transfer the pizza to a baking sheet or pizza stone and bake for about 10-12 minutes, or until the crust is golden and the cheese is melted and bubbly.
11. Remove from the oven, let it cool for a few minutes, then slice and serve.

Nutritional Value (Amount per Serving):

Calories: 1275; Fat: 63.98; Carb: 118.85; Protein: 59.12

Chicken and Chourico Pizza

Prep Time: 25 Mins   Cook Time: 30 Mins   Serves: 6

Ingredients:

- 2 teaspoons olive oil
- 2 skinless, boneless chicken breast halves cut into small chunks
- flour for dusting
- 1 (13.4 ounce) package room-temperature fresh pizza dough
- 1 cup tomato sauce
- 1 tablespoon olive oil
- 5 cloves garlic, minced
- 1 ½ tablespoons Italian seasoning
- salt and ground black pepper to taste
- ½ link Portuguese hot chourico sausage halved lengthwise and sliced into thin half moons
- ¼ red onion, sliced thin
- ¼ cup banana pepper rings
- 1 (8 ounce) package shredded mozzarella & cheddar pizza cheese
- 2 tablespoons grated Parmesan cheese

Directions:

1. Preheat an oven. Prepare a pizza pan with olive oil and flour.

2. Heat 2 teaspoons olive oil in a skillet over medium heat; cook the chicken in the hot oil until no longer pink in the center and the juices run clear, 5 to 10 minutes. Set aside.
3. Dust a flat working surface with flour. Roll the pizza dough out to the size of your pizza pan. Place dough on the prepared pan.
4. Stir the tomato sauce, 1 tablespoon olive oil, garlic, Italian seasoning, salt, and pepper together in a small bowl; spread evenly over the surface of the dough. Scatter, in order, the chicken, chourico, red onion, banana peppers, pizza cheese, and Parmesan over the tomato sauce mixture.
5. Bake in the preheated oven until the cheese is lightly browned, about 20 minutes.

Nutritional Value (Amount per Serving):

Calories: 793; Fat: 24.44; Carb: 93.6; Protein: 46.83

Broccoli Rabe, Garlic Smoked Mozzarella Pizza

Prep Time: 5 Mins   Cook Time: 20 Mins   Serves: 4

Ingredients:

- 1 pizza dough
- 2 cups broccoli rabe, blanched and chopped
- 3 cloves garlic, minced
- 2 tablespoons olive oil
- 1 cup shredded smoked mozzarella cheese
- Salt and pepper to taste
- Red pepper flakes (optional)

Directions:

1. Preheat your oven.
2. Roll out the pizza dough on a floured surface to your desired thickness.
3. Place the dough on a baking sheet or pizza stone.
4. In a skillet, heat the olive oil over medium heat. Add the minced garlic and cook for 1-2 minutes until fragrant.
5. Add the blanched and chopped broccoli rabe to the skillet and sauté for an additional 2-3 minutes.
6. Season with salt, pepper, and red pepper flakes if desired.
7. Spread the broccoli rabe mixture evenly over the pizza dough.
8. Top with shredded smoked mozzarella cheese.
9. Bake in the preheated oven for 12-15 minutes or until the crust is golden and the cheese is melted and bubbly.
10. Remove from the oven, let it cool slightly, and then slice and serve.

Calories: 503; Fat: 19.99; Carb: 53.31; Protein: 28.57

Turkey and Artichoke Pizza

Prep Time: 15 Mins   Cook Time: 15 Mins   Serves: 4

Ingredients:

- 1 pre-made pizza dough
- 1/2 cup tomato sauce
- 1 cup shredded cooked turkey
- 1 cup marinated artichoke hearts, drained and chopped
- 1 cup shredded mozzarella cheese
- 1/4 cup sliced black olives
- Fresh basil leaves, for garnish

Directions:

1. Preheat your oven to the temperature recommended on the pizza dough package.
2. Roll out the pizza dough on a floured surface to your desired thickness.
3. Transfer the dough to a baking sheet or pizza stone.
4. Spread the tomato sauce evenly over the dough.
5. Sprinkle the shredded turkey, chopped artichoke hearts, mozzarella cheese, and black olives on top.
6. Bake in the preheated oven for the recommended time or until the crust is golden and the cheese is melted and bubbly.
7. Remove from the oven and garnish with fresh basil leaves before serving.

Nutritional Value (Amount per Serving):

Calories: 645; Fat: 46.7; Carb: 23.43; Protein: 31.49

Popcorn Shrimp Pizza

Prep Time: 15 Mins   Cook Time: 15 Mins   Serves: 8

Ingredients:

- 2 cups Popcorn shrimp
- 2 cups Mozzarella cheese
- 1 cup Tomato sauce
- ¼ cup Parsley
- ½ lb. Raw shrimp deshelled and deveined
- 1 Egg
- 1 cup Panko breadcrumbs
- ½ cup Flour
- 1 tsp Salt
- 1 tsp Garlic powder
- 1 tsp Onion powder

- 1 tsp Paprika
- 1 tsp Oregano
- 1 tsp Thyme
- ½ tsp Black pepper

Directions:

1. Preheat oven. Deshell and devein raw shrimps.
2. Get 3 mixing bowls. Add flour, garlic powder, onion powder, paprika, oregano, thyme, salt and black pepper to mixing bowl #1. Add egg to a mixing bowl #2 and mix lightly. And add breadcrumbs to mixing bowl #3.
3. Add shrimps to flour mixing bowl and coat evenly. Then add shrimps to egg mixing bowl and coat evenly. Finally add shrimps to the breadcrumb mixing bowl coating evenly. Then put shrimps single file onto a parchment paper lined baking tray and bake 400°F for 5 minutes. Flip shrimps and cook an additional 5 minutes, remove from oven.
4. Turn up the oven temperature.
5. Flour surface and roll out the dough. Put a floured pizza peel underneath the dough. Add tomato sauce to pizza, then top with mozzarella cheese. Add popcorn shrimp. Pat down the toppings before putting into the oven.
6. Bake pizza in the oven for 8-10 minutes. Let cool 5 minutes then slice it up!

Nutritional Value (Amount per Serving):

Calories: 195; Fat: 2.66; Carb: 22.22; Protein: 19.03

Shrimp and Grits Pizza

Prep Time: 10 Mins   Cook Time: 35 Mins   Serves: 8

Ingredients:

- 1½ cup Shrimp
- 1 cup Grits
- 1 cup Bacon
- 2 cups Mozzarella cheese
- ¼ cup Green onion
- 1 tbsp Garlic (2 cloves)
- 1 tbsp Butter
- ½ cup Grits (or Cornmeal)
- 1 cup Water
- 1 cup Milk
- ¼ cup Cheddar cheese
- 2 tbsp Butter
- 1 tsp Salt
- ½ tsp Black pepper `

Directions:

1. In saucepan, bring milk and water to boil over medium heat, whisk often. Slowly whisk in grits then turn heat to low and cover.
2. Remove lid every 5 minutes to whisk. Cook for a total of 20 minutes or until creamy.
3. Remove from heat, add salt, pepper and butter then whisk. Add cheese and whisk until smooth.
4. Bake bacon in oven on parchment paper lined baking pan at 420°F for 15 minutes, then flip. Cook bacon an additional 5-10 minutes, or until cooked

(make sure not to overcook it because it will be cooking in the oven for an additional 10 minutes on the pizza).

5. Remove bacon and drain on paper towel lined plate. Let cool, then chop into bite sized pieces, reserve 1 cup.
6. Dice garlic. In frying pan cook butter, garlic and shrimp on medium-high heat for 1 minute each side, turn off heat and remove from pan.
7. Preheat oven with baking steel or pizza stone inside the oven.
8. Flour surface and roll out the dough. Put a floured pizza peel underneath the dough.
9. Add warm grits, 1 cup mozzarella cheese, bacon, shrimps, 1 cup mozzarella cheese, green onions. Pat down the toppings before putting into the oven.
10. Bake pizza at 550°F for 8-10 minutes, by sliding pizza onto baking steel with pizza peel.
11. Remove pizza from oven with pizza peel. Let cool for 5 minutes, slice and enjoy!

Nutritional Value (Amount per Serving):

Calories: 211; Fat: 11.41; Carb: 10.36; Protein: 17.85

Deep-Dish Pizza with Mushrooms, Red Onion Kale

Prep Time: 20 Mins   Cook Time: 45 Mins   Serves: 4

Ingredients:

- 1 pound pizza dough
- 1 tablespoon olive oil
- 1 red onion, thinly sliced
- 8 ounces mushrooms, sliced
- 2 cups chopped kale
- 1 cup marinara sauce
- 2 cups shredded mozzarella cheese
- Salt and pepper to taste

Directions:

1. Preheat the oven.
2. In a large skillet, heat olive oil over medium heat.
3. Add the sliced red onion and mushrooms to the skillet and sauté until softened, about 5-7 minutes.
4. Add the chopped kale to the skillet and cook for an additional 2-3 minutes, until wilted.
5. Season with salt and pepper to taste.
6. Roll out the pizza dough and press it into a deep-dish pizza pan, covering the bottom and sides.
7. Spread the marinara sauce evenly over the dough.
8. Sprinkle half of the shredded mozzarella cheese over the sauce.
9. Spread the sautéed onion, mushrooms, and kale mixture over the cheese.
10. Top with the remaining shredded mozzarella cheese.

11. Bake in the preheated oven for about 30-35 minutes, or until the crust is golden and the cheese is melted and bubbly.
12. Remove from the oven and let it cool for a few minutes before slicing and serving.

Nutritional Value (Amount per Serving):

Calories: 486; Fat: 21.01; Carb: 42.5; Protein: 33.97

Crescent Roll Veggie Pizza

Prep Time: 10 Mins   Cook Time: 25 Mins   Serves: 10

Ingredients:

- 2 tubes Pillsbury crescent dough sheets or crescent rolls 8 ounces each
- 12 ounces cream cheese softened
- ¾ cup sour cream
- 1 teaspoon dried dill weed
- 2 teaspoons sliced fresh chives
- ¼ teaspoon garlic powder
- ¼ teaspoon crush red pepper red pepper flakes
- 1 teaspoon kosher salt
- ½ teaspoon freshly ground black pepper
- ¼ cup diced red onion
- 1 cup tomatoes diced
- ¾ cup bell peppers yellow, red & orange
- ½ cup shredded peeled carrots
- ¼ cup thinly sliced radishes
- ½ cup diced broccoli
- ½ cup diced cauliflower

Directions:

1. Heat oven and lightly spray a large rimmed baking sheet with nonstick cooking spray.
2. Remove the dough from the refrigerator 5 minutes before using. Set the dough in the pan and press it over the bottom and halfway up the sides. Pinch the seams of the dough together. Refrigerate the dough 5-10 minutes before baking.
3. Bake the crust for 15-20 minutes or until a little darker than golden brown and is cooked through. Cool Completely.
4. While the crust cooks, beat together cream cheese, sour cream, dill, chives, garlic, crushed red pepper, salt and pepper.
5. Once the crust has cooled, spread the cream cheese/sour cream mixture evenly over the crust. Top the pizza with the vegetables, and lightly press

them into the cream cheese layer.

6. Serve immediately, or cover lightly with plastic wrap and refrigerate up to 24 hours.

Calories: 201; Fat: 15.5; Carb: 7.6; Protein: 8.34

Turkey and Bacon Ranch Pizza

Prep Time: 15 Mins   Cook Time: 15 Mins   Serves: 4

Ingredients:

- 1 pre-made pizza dough
- 1/4 cup ranch dressing
- 1 cup shredded cooked turkey
- 1 cup shredded mozzarella cheese
- 4 slices cooked bacon, crumbled
- 1/4 cup sliced green onions

Directions:

1. Preheat your oven to the temperature recommended on the pizza dough package.
2. Roll out the pizza dough on a floured surface to your desired thickness.
3. Transfer the dough to a baking sheet or pizza stone.
4. Spread the ranch dressing evenly over the dough.
5. Sprinkle the shredded turkey, mozzarella cheese, crumbled bacon, and sliced green onions on top.
6. Bake in the preheated oven for the recommended time or until the crust is golden and the cheese is melted and bubbly.
7. Remove from the oven and let it cool for a few minutes before slicing and serving.

Nutritional Value (Amount per Serving):

Calories: 748; Fat: 62.47; Carb: 12.46; Protein: 32.85

Mac-N-Cheese Pizza

Prep Time: 25 Mins   Cook Time: 30 Mins   Serves: 4

Ingredients:

- cooking spray
- 1 (11 ounce) package refrigerated pizza crust
- 1 ½ cups elbow macaroni
- ¼ cup butter
- 1 tablespoon all-purpose flour
- milk

- ¾ pound processed cheese, cubed
- ½ cup shredded mozzarella cheese

1. Preheat oven. Spray a baking sheet with cooking spray. Unroll pizza crust and place on the prepared baking pan.
2. Bring a large pot of lightly salted water to a boil. Cook elbow macaroni in the boiling water, stirring occasionally until cooked through but firm to the bite, 8 minutes. Drain.
3. Melt butter in a large saucepan over medium heat; cook and stir flour with butter until it has a slightly toasted fragrance, about 2 minutes. Whisk in milk and simmer until thickened, whisking constantly, 2 more minutes. Stir in processed cheese cubes. Let the cheese cubes melt, stirring often, to make a smooth cheese sauce.
4. Spread about 3/4 cup of cheese sauce onto the pizza crust. Stir cooked macaroni into remaining cheese sauce in the saucepan and spoon the macaroni and cheese onto the crust in an even layer. Sprinkle top of pizza with mozzarella cheese.
5. Bake in the preheated oven until the crust is lightly browned and the mozzarella cheese is golden brown, about 15 minutes.

Nutritional Value (Amount per Serving):

Calories: 652; Fat: 36.83; Carb: 51.07; Protein: 29.26

Turkey and Cranberry Pizza

Prep Time: 15 Mins   Cook Time: 10 Mins   Serves: 4

Ingredients:

- 1 pre-made pizza dough
- 1/2 cup cranberry sauce
- 1 cup shredded cooked turkey
- 1 cup shredded mozzarella cheese
- 1/4 cup chopped fresh parsley

Directions:

1. Preheat your oven to the temperature recommended on the pizza dough package.
2. Roll out the pizza dough on a floured surface to your desired thickness.
3. Transfer the dough to a baking sheet or pizza stone.
4. Spread the cranberry sauce evenly over the dough.
5. Sprinkle the shredded turkey and mozzarella cheese on top.
6. Bake in the preheated oven for the recommended time or until the crust is golden and the cheese is melted and bubbly.
7. Remove from the oven and sprinkle with chopped fresh parsley before serving.

Calories: 631; Fat: 45.64; Carb: 24.84; Protein: 29.53

Turkey Pesto Pizza

Prep Time: 15 Mins   Cook Time: 10 Mins   Serves: 4

Ingredients:

- 1 pre-made pizza dough
- 1/2 cup pesto sauce
- 1 cup shredded cooked turkey
- 1 cup shredded mozzarella cheese
- 1/4 cup sliced sun-dried tomatoes
- Fresh basil leaves, for garnish

Directions:

1. Preheat your oven to the temperature recommended on the pizza dough package.
2. Roll out the pizza dough on a floured surface to your desired thickness.
3. Transfer the dough to a baking sheet or pizza stone.
4. Spread the pesto sauce evenly over the dough.
5. Sprinkle the shredded turkey, mozzarella cheese, and sun-dried tomatoes on top.
6. Bake in the preheated oven for the recommended time or until the crust is golden and the cheese is melted and bubbly.
7. Remove from the oven and garnish with fresh basil leaves before serving.

Nutritional Value (Amount per Serving):

Calories: 596; Fat: 45.71; Carb: 15.2; Protein: 30.33

Puff Pastry Margherita Pizza

Prep Time: 15 Mins   Cook Time: 18 Mins   Serves: 4

Ingredients:

- 2 sheets frozen puff pastry, thawed
- 1 large egg
- 1 tablespoon water
- 1 (14.5 ounce can) whole peeled tomatoes, drained
- 2 teaspoons extra-virgin olive oil, divided
- 1 clove garlic
- 1 pinch sea salt
- 6 ounces fresh mozzarella cheese, chopped
- 1/4 cup shredded Parmigiano-Reggiano cheese
- 10 basil leaves, torn

1. Preheat the oven. Spread each sheet of puff pastry onto a piece of lightly floured parchment paper. Use a rolling pin to roll pastry into even rectangles. Lift pastry (with parchment paper) onto baking sheets.
2. Pierce puff pastry all over with a fork. Beat egg with water in a small dish; brush pastry all over with egg wash.
3. Bake in the preheated oven for 10 minutes.
4. Meanwhile, pulse tomatoes, 1/2 teaspoon of the olive oil, garlic, and a pinch of salt together in a food processor until pureed.
5. Carefully press pastry crusts down to deflate them. Spread half the tomato sauce evenly to within about an inch of edges of each crust; drizzle with remaining olive oil. Top evenly with mozzarella cheese and Parmigiano-Reggiano cheese.
6. Bake until cheese is melted and crust edges are golden, about 5 more minutes. Remove from the oven and scatter basil leaves over the top. Slice and serve hot.

Nutritional Value (Amount per Serving):

Calories: 346; Fat: 14.6; Carb: 36.65; Protein: 22.79

Fresh Pesto Pizza

Prep Time: 15 Mins   Cook Time: 10 Mins   Serves: 8

Ingredients:

- 1 (12 inch) pre-baked whole-wheat pizza crust
- 1 cup prepared pesto
- 1 ½ cups chopped fresh spinach
- 1 tomato, chopped
- 1 cup shredded mozzarella cheese
- ½ cup crumbled feta cheese

Directions:

1. Preheat oven.
2. Remove crust from wrapper and spread pesto over crust; top with a layer of spinach leaves, chopped tomato, shredded mozzarella cheese and feta cheese. Place pizza on a baking sheet.
3. Bake pizza in the preheated oven until the spinach leaves are wilted and the cheese is melted, bubbling, and beginning to brown, 10 to 12 minutes.

Nutritional Value (Amount per Serving):

Calories: 236; Fat: 19.15; Carb: 7.56; Protein: 10.06

Basic Vegetable Pizza

Prep Time: 15 Mins   Cook Time: 1 Hr 30 Mins   Serves: 4

Ingredients:

- 2 (8 ounce) packages refrigerated crescent rolls
- 2 (8 ounce) packages cream cheese, softened
- 1 cup mayonnaise
- 1 (1 ounce) package dry Ranch-style dressing mix
- 1 cup fresh broccoli, chopped
- 1 cup chopped tomatoes
- 1 cup chopped green bell pepper
- 1 cup chopped cauliflower
- 1 cup shredded carrots
- 1 cup shredded Cheddar cheese

Directions:

1. Gather all ingredients.
2. Preheat the oven.
3. Roll out crescent roll dough onto a baking sheet, and pinch together edges to form the pizza crust.
4. Bake crust in the preheated oven for 12 minutes. Once finished cooking, remove crust from the oven and let cool for about 15 minutes without removing it from the baking sheet.
5. Combine cream cheese, mayonnaise, and dry Ranch dressing mix in a small mixing bowl. Spread the mixture over the cooled crust.
6. Arrange broccoli, tomatoes, bell pepper, cauliflower, shredded carrots, and Cheddar cheese over the cream cheese layer.
7. Chill for 1 hour, slice, and serve .

Nutritional Value (Amount per Serving):

Calories: 469; Fat: 55.15; Carb: 24.22; Protein: 14.51

Chicken Pesto Pizza with Roasted Red Peppers and Asparagus

Prep Time: 10 Mins   Cook Time: 15 Mins   Serves: 6

Ingredients:

- 1 (10 ounce) can premium white-meat chicken, packed in water, drained
- ⅓ cup diced onion
- 2 cloves garlic, minced
- 2 tablespoons olive oil

- 4 tablespoons basil pesto sauce, divided
- 1 serving Vegetable oil spray
- 1 (10 ounce) package refrigerated pizza dough
- 1 cup fresh asparagus cut in 1-inch pieces, or canned, cut asparagus, drained
- 1 cup chopped, fresh red bell peppers (roasted) or canned, roasted red bell peppers, drained
- ½ cup shredded part-skim mozzarella cheese
- 1 ounce feta cheese, crumbled

Directions:

1. Heat oven. Brown chicken with onion and garlic in olive oil in a medium, non-stick skillet.
2. Remove from heat; blend with 2 tablespoons pesto sauce; set aside.
3. Lightly coat a baking sheet or a pizza stone with vegetable oil spray.
4. Press or roll dough onto baking sheet or pizza stone to desired thickness.
5. Spread remaining 2 tablespoons pesto sauce over dough, leaving a 1-inch edge.
6. Arrange chicken mixture, asparagus and roasted red peppers on top.
7. Sprinkle with cheeses. Bake for 12 to 15 minutes until cheeses melt and crust is lightly browned.

Nutritional Value (Amount per Serving):

Calories: 438; Fat: 24.63; Carb: 38.21; Protein: 17.3

Crescent Roll Vegetable Pizza

Prep Time: 45 Mins   Cook Time: 8 Hrs 40 Mins   Serves: 8

Ingredients:

- 2 (8 ounce) packages refrigerated crescent rolls
- 2 (8 ounce) packages cream cheese, softened
- ⅓ cup mayonnaise
- 1 (1.4 ounce) package dry vegetable soup mix (such as Knorr)
- 1 cup radishes, sliced
- ⅓ cup chopped green bell pepper
- ⅓ cup chopped red bell pepper
- ⅓ cup chopped yellow bell pepper
- 1 cup broccoli florets
- 1 cup cauliflower florets
- ½ cup chopped carrot
- ½ cup chopped celery

Directions:

1. Preheat the oven.

2. Spread crescent roll dough out into an jelly roll pan; pinch perforations and seams together to make a crust.
3. Bake in the preheated oven until crust is lightly golden brown, about 10 minutes. Let cool completely, about 30 minutes.
4. Mix cream cheese, mayonnaise, and vegetable soup mix together in a bowl. Spread cream cheese mixture over the crust. Sprinkle pizza with radishes, bell peppers, broccoli, cauliflower, carrot, and celery, pressing vegetables into the cream cheese mixture.
5. Cut pizza into squares, cover with plastic wrap, and refrigerate 8 hours to overnight to blend flavors.

Nutritional Value (Amount per Serving):

Calories: 250; Fat: 20.83; Carb: 10.19; Protein: 6.58

Chicken and Cranberry Pizza with Brie and Almonds

Prep Time: 25 Mins   Cook Time: 10 Mins   Serves: 6

Ingredients:

- 1 (12 inch) pre-baked Italian pizza crust
- 1 ½ cups whole-berry cranberry sauce from a 16-ounce can
- 2 cups shredded chicken
- 4 ounces Brie, cut into small chunks
- 3 green onions, thinly sliced
- ¼ cup slivered almonds
- 1 cup shredded mozzarella

Directions:

1. Heat oven to 450 degrees.
2. Place crust on a cookie sheet, and spread 1 cup of cranberry sauce over the crust. Toss remaining 1/2 cup with chicken. Top pizza with chicken, brie, green onions, almonds and mozzarella. Bake until the crust is crisp and cheese melts, 10 to 12 minutes.
3. Cut into 6 slices and serve.

Nutritional Value (Amount per Serving):

Calories: 494; Fat: 16.55; Carb: 6.92; Protein: 75.6

Garden Veggie Pizza Squares

Prep Time: 5 Mins   Cook Time: 1 Hr 15 Mins   Serves: 4

Ingredients:

- 1 (8 ounce) package refrigerated crescent rolls

- 1 (8 ounce) package cream cheese, softened
- 1 (1 ounce) package Ranch-style dressing mix
- 2 carrots, finely chopped
- ½ cup chopped red bell peppers
- ½ cup chopped green bell pepper
- ½ cup fresh broccoli, chopped
- ½ cup chopped green onions

Directions:

1. Preheat the oven.
2. Roll out crescent rolls onto a large nonstick baking sheet. Stretch and flatten to form a single rectangular shape on the baking sheet.
3. Bake in the preheated oven until golden brown, 11 to 13 minutes. Allow to cool.
4. Mix cream cheese with 1/2 of the ranch dressing mix in a medium bowl; add more dressing mix to taste. Spread mixture over cooled crust.
5. Arrange carrots, bell peppers, broccoli, and green onions on top. Chill in the refrigerator for about 1 hour. Cut into 48 bite-sized squares to serve.

Nutritional Value (Amount per Serving):

Calories: 230; Fat: 17.76; Carb: 12.31; Protein: 6.34

Gourmet Chicken Pizza

Prep Time: 15 Mins   Cook Time: 40 Mins   Serves: 8

Ingredients:

- 2 skinless, boneless chicken breast halves
- 1 (10 ounce) can refrigerated pizza crust
- ½ cup Ranch-style salad dressing
- 1 cup shredded mozzarella cheese
- 1 cup shredded Cheddar cheese
- 1 cup chopped tomatoes
- ¼ cup chopped green onions

Directions:

1. Preheat oven. Lightly grease a pizza pan or medium baking sheet.
2. Place chicken in a large skillet over medium-high heat. Cook until no longer pink, and juices run clear. Cool, then either shred or chop into small pieces.
3. Unroll dough, and press into the prepared pizza pan or baking sheet. Bake crust for 7 minutes in the preheated oven, or until it begins to turn golden brown. Remove from oven.
4. Spread ranch dressing over partially baked crust. Sprinkle on mozzarella cheese. Place tomatoes, green onion, and chicken on top of mozzarella

cheese, then top with Cheddar cheese. Return to the oven for 20 to 25 minutes, until cheese is melted and bubbly.

Nutritional Value (Amount per Serving):

Calories: 321; Fat: 16.64; Carb: 17.74; Protein: 24.49

Pizza Pizzettes

Prep Time: 20 Mins   Cook Time: 15 Mins   Serves: 6

Ingredients:

- 1 pound pizza dough
- 1/2 cup marinara sauce
- 1 cup shredded mozzarella cheese
- Toppings of your choice (e.g., sliced pepperoni, olives, mushrooms, bell peppers, etc.)

Directions:

1. Preheat the oven.
2. Divide the pizza dough into small portions and roll them out into mini pizza rounds.
3. Place the mini pizza rounds on a baking sheet lined with parchment paper.
4. Spread a thin layer of marinara sauce on each mini pizza round.
5. Sprinkle shredded mozzarella cheese over the sauce.
6. Add your desired toppings to each pizzette.
7. Bake in the preheated oven for about 10-15 minutes, or until the crust is golden and the cheese is melted and bubbly.
8. Remove from the oven and let them cool for a few minutes before serving.

Nutritional Value (Amount per Serving):

Calories: 260; Fat: 11.54; Carb: 24.38; Protein: 14.93

Chapter 5: Poultry and Seafood Pizzas

Savory Seafood Pizza

Prep Time: 25 Mins   Cook Time: 1 Hr 45 Mins   Serves: 4-8

Ingredients:

- cooking spray
- 1 (10 ounce) package refrigerated pizza dough
- 3 tablespoons crushed dried rosemary
- 2 teaspoons cornmeal for dusting
- 1 teaspoon butter
- 1 teaspoon all-purpose flour
- ¼ cup half-and-half
- ¼ cup white cooking wine
- 2 tablespoons grated Parmesan cheese
- hot sauce
- 12 ounces imitation crabmeat, flaked
- 2 cups shredded mozzarella cheese
- ½ cup shredded zucchini
- ½ cup sliced fresh mushrooms
- 10 pitted black olives, halved

Directions:

1. Spray a large bowl with cooking spray. Coat pizza dough with spray and rosemary; place into the bowl. Cover with a towel and let rise in a warm place until doubled in volume, about 1 hour.
2. Spray a baking sheet with cooking spray; lightly dust with cornmeal. Stretch the dough onto the sheet until it covers the bottom and dangles over the edge.
3. Preheat oven.
4. Melt butter in a small saucepan over medium heat. Mix in flour until creamy. Add half-and-half; cook, stirring constantly, until thickened, about 3 minutes. Add wine, Parmesan cheese, and hot sauce; cook and stir until thick and creamy, about 5 minutes. Remove sauce from heat; cool until just slightly warm, at least 8 minutes.
5. Spread sauce onto the pizza dough to form a thin, even layer. Cover with pieces of crab meat; layer 1 1/2 cups mozzarella cheese, zucchini, mushrooms, and olives on top. Cover with the remaining mozzarella cheese.
6. Bake pizza in the preheated oven for 5 minutes. Reduce heat; bake until golden brown, 25 more minutes.

Nutritional Value (Amount per Serving):

Calories: 569; Fat: 28.91; Carb: 38.28; Protein: 39.64

Mediterranean Shrimp Pizza

Prep Time: 20 Mins   Cook Time: 20 Mins   Serves: 4

Ingredients:

- 1 pre-made pizza dough
- 2 tablespoons olive oil
- 3 cloves garlic, minced
- 1 cup baby spinach leaves
- 1 cup shredded mozzarella cheese
- 1/2 cup cooked shrimp, peeled and deveined
- 1/4 cup sliced Kalamata olives
- 1/4 cup crumbled feta cheese
- 2 tablespoons chopped fresh basil

Directions:

1. Preheat your oven to the temperature recommended on the pizza dough package.
2. Heat the olive oil in a skillet over medium heat.
3. Add the minced garlic and cook for 1-2 minutes until fragrant.
4. Add the baby spinach leaves to the skillet and cook until wilted, about 2-3 minutes.
5. Roll out the pizza dough on a floured surface to your desired thickness.
6. Transfer the dough to a baking sheet or pizza stone.
7. Spread the cooked garlic and spinach mixture evenly over the dough.
8. Sprinkle the shredded mozzarella cheese on top.
9. Arrange the cooked shrimps, sliced Kalamata olives, and crumbled feta cheese on the pizza.
10. Bake in the preheated oven for the recommended time or until the crust is golden and the cheese is melted and bubbly.
11. Remove from the oven and sprinkle with chopped fresh basil before serving.

Nutritional Value (Amount per Serving):

Calories: 221; Fat: 11.9; Carb: 13.09; Protein: 15.77

Lox Bagel Pizza

Prep Time: 10 Mins   Cook Time: 15 Mins   Serves: 4

Ingredients:

- 1 pizza dough
- 16 slices Lox
- 2 cups Mozzarella cheese
- 1 cup Plain cream cheese
- ½ cup Red onion
- 2 tbsp Capers

Directions:

1. Preheat oven with baking steel or pizza stone inside the oven.
2. Grate mozzarella cheese.

3. Thinly slice red onions.
4. Flour surface and roll out the dough. Put a floured pizza peel underneath the dough.
5. Add cream cheese, then mozzarella cheese. Pat down the toppings before putting into the oven.
6. Bake pizza for 8-10 minutes, by sliding pizza onto baking steel with pizza peel.
7. Remove pizza from oven with pizza peel. Let cool for 5 minutes. Add 2 slices of Lox to each slice, then add onions and capers.

Nutritional Value (Amount per Serving):

Calories: 756; Fat: 36.49; Carb: 57.07; Protein: 50.79

Duck and Mushroom Pizza

Prep Time: 20 Mins   Cook Time: 20 Mins   Serves: 4

Ingredients:

- 1 pre-made pizza dough
- 1/2 cup tomato sauce
- 1 cup shredded cooked duck
- 1 cup sliced mushrooms
- 1 cup shredded mozzarella cheese
- 2 tablespoons chopped fresh thyme

Directions:

1. Preheat your oven to the temperature recommended on the pizza dough package.
2. Roll out the pizza dough on a floured surface to your desired thickness.
3. Transfer the dough to a baking sheet or pizza stone.
4. Spread the tomato sauce evenly over the dough.
5. Sprinkle the shredded duck, sliced mushrooms, mozzarella cheese, and chopped fresh thyme on top.
6. Bake in the preheated oven for the recommended time or until the crust is golden and the cheese is melted and bubbly.
7. Remove from the oven and let it cool for a few minutes before slicing and serving.

Nutritional Value (Amount per Serving):

Calories: 365; Fat: 14.5; Carb: 18.23; Protein: 37.61

Chicken and Artichoke Pizza

Prep Time: 15 Mins   Cook Time: 15 Mins   Serves: 4

Ingredients:

- 1 pound pizza dough

- 1/2 cup pizza sauce
- 2 cups shredded mozzarella cheese
- 1 cup cooked chicken breast, diced
- 1 cup marinated artichoke hearts, drained and chopped
- 1/4 cup sliced black olives
- 2 tablespoons chopped fresh basil

Directions:

1. Preheat the oven.
2. Roll out the pizza dough on a floured surface to your desired thickness.
3. Transfer the rolled-out dough to a pizza stone or baking sheet.
4. Spread the pizza sauce evenly over the dough.
5. Sprinkle shredded mozzarella cheese over the sauce.
6. Arrange the cooked chicken, artichoke hearts, and black olives on top of the cheese.
7. Bake in the preheated oven for about 12-15 minutes, or until the crust is golden and the cheese is melted and bubbly.
8. Remove from the oven and sprinkle chopped fresh basil over the pizza.
9. Let it cool for a few minutes, slice, and serve.

Nutritional Value (Amount per Serving):

Calories: 522; Fat: 19.9; Carb: 42.62; Protein: 43.49

Butternut Squash Pizzas with Rosemary

Prep Time: 20 Mins   Cook Time: 30 Mins   Serves: 8

Ingredients:

- 1 cup thinly sliced onion
- ½ butternut squash peeled, seeded, and thinly sliced
- 1 teaspoon chopped fresh rosemary
- salt and black pepper to taste
- 3 tablespoons olive oil, divided
- 1 (16 ounce) package refrigerated pizza crust dough, divided
- 1 tablespoon cornmeal
- 2 tablespoons grated Asiago or Parmesan cheese

Directions:

1. Preheat the oven. Place sliced onion and squash in a roasting pan. Sprinkle with rosemary, salt, pepper, and 2 tablespoons of olive oil; toss to coat.
2. Bake in the preheated oven for 20 minutes, or until onions are lightly browned and squash is tender; set aside.
3. Increase oven temperature.
4. Roll each ball of dough into an 8-inch round on a lightly floured surface.

Place each round on a baking sheet sprinkled with cornmeal; distribute squash mixture over the two rounds and bake in the preheated oven for 10 minutes, checking occasionally, or until the crust is firm. Sprinkle with cheese and remaining tablespoon olive oil. Cut into quarters, and serve.

Nutritional Value (Amount per Serving):

Calories: 1044; Fat: 56.55; Carb: 93.06; Protein: 40.73

Grilled Veggie Pizza

Prep Time: 10 Mins   Cook Time: 20 Mins   Serves: 6

Ingredients:

- 8 small fresh mushrooms, halved
- 1 small zucchini, cut into 1/4-inch slices
- 1 small sweet yellow pepper, sliced
- 1 small sweet red pepper, sliced
- 1 small onion, sliced
- 1 tablespoon white wine vinegar
- 1 tablespoon water
- 4 teaspoons olive oil, divided
- 2 teaspoons minced fresh basil or 1/2 teaspoon dried basil
- 1/4 teaspoon salt
- 1/4 teaspoon pepper
- 1 prebaked thin whole wheat pizza crust
- 1 can (8 ounces) pizza sauce
- 2 small tomatoes, chopped
- 2 cups shredded part-skim mozzarella cheese

Directions:

1. In a large bowl, combine the mushrooms, zucchini, peppers, onion, vinegar, water, 3 teaspoons oil and seasonings. Transfer to a grill wok or basket. Grill, covered, over medium heat for 8-10 minutes or until tender, stirring once.
2. Prepare grill for indirect heat. Brush crust with remaining oil; spread with pizza sauce. Top with grilled vegetables, tomatoes and cheese. Grill, covered, over indirect medium heat for 10-12 minutes or until edges are lightly browned and cheese is melted. Rotate pizza halfway through cooking to ensure an evenly browned crust.

Nutritional Value (Amount per Serving):

Calories: 434; Fat: 20.52; Carb: 40.33; Protein: 22.75

Homemade Mushroom Pizza

Prep Time: 15 Mins   Cook Time: 10 Mins   Serves: 4

Ingredients:

- 1 (12 inch) pre-baked pizza crust
- 3 tablespoons olive oil
- 1 teaspoon sesame oil or to taste
- 1 cup fresh spinach, rinsed and dried
- 8 ounces shredded mozzarella cheese
- 1 cup sliced fresh mushrooms

Directions:

1. Preheat the oven. Place pizza crust on a baking sheet.
2. In a small bowl, mix together olive oil and sesame oil. Brush onto pre-baked pizza crust, covering the entire surface. Stack spinach leaves, then cut lengthwise into 1/2-inch strips; scatter evenly over crust. Cover pizza with shredded mozzarella, and top with sliced mushrooms.
3. Bake in the preheated oven for 8 to 10 minutes, or until cheese is melted and edges are crisp.

Nutritional Value (Amount per Serving):

Calories: 498; Fat: 27.55; Carb: 32.81; Protein: 30.23

Artichoke, Spinach Olive Tapenade Pizza

Prep Time: 15 Mins   Cook Time: 15 Mins   Serves: 4

Ingredients:

- 1 pizza dough
- 1/2 cup olive tapenade
- 1 cup chopped artichoke hearts (canned or marinated)
- 1 cup chopped fresh spinach
- 1 cup shredded mozzarella cheese
- 1/4 cup crumbled feta cheese
- Red pepper flakes (optional)

Directions:

1. Preheat your oven to the highest temperature.
2. Roll out the pizza dough into a thin circle on a floured surface.
3. Spread the olive tapenade evenly over the pizza dough.
4. Scatter the chopped artichoke hearts and fresh spinach over the tapenade.
5. Sprinkle the shredded mozzarella cheese over the toppings.
6. Crumble the feta cheese over the mozzarella.
7. If desired, sprinkle some red pepper flakes for a spicy kick.
8. Transfer the pizza to a baking sheet or pizza stone and bake for about 10-12 minutes, or until the crust is golden and the cheese is melted and bubbly.

9. Remove from the oven, let it cool for a few minutes, then slice and serve.

Nutritional Value (Amount per Serving):

Calories: 496; Fat: 16.99; Carb: 56.9; Protein: 30.58

Roasted Squash, Smoked Mozzarella Sage

Prep Time: 15 Mins   Cook Time: 30 Mins   Serves: 4

Ingredients:

- 1 small butternut squash, peeled, seeded, and cut into 1/2-inch cubes
- 2 tablespoons olive oil
- Salt and pepper to taste
- 1 pound pizza dough
- 1 cup shredded smoked mozzarella cheese
- 8-10 fresh sage leaves

Directions:

1. Preheat the oven.
2. In a bowl, toss the butternut squash cubes with olive oil, salt, and pepper.
3. Spread the squash evenly on a baking sheet and roast in the preheated oven for about 20-25 minutes, or until tender and slightly caramelized.
4. Meanwhile, roll out the pizza dough on a floured surface to your desired thickness.
5. Transfer the rolled-out dough to a baking sheet or pizza stone.
6. Sprinkle the shredded smoked mozzarella cheese evenly over the dough.
7. Arrange the roasted butternut squash cubes on top of the cheese.
8. Tear the sage leaves into smaller pieces and scatter them over the pizza.
9. Bake in the preheated oven for about 15-20 minutes, or until the crust is golden and the cheese is melted and bubbly.
10. Remove from the oven and let it cool for a few minutes before slicing and serving.

Nutritional Value (Amount per Serving):

Calories: 459; Fat: 24.64; Carb: 38.1; Protein: 22.78

Teriyaki Chicken and Vegetable Pizza

Prep Time: 20 Mins   Cook Time: 15 Mins   Serves: 4

Ingredients:

- 1 pound pizza dough
- 1/4 cup teriyaki sauce
- 2 cups shredded mozzarella cheese
- 1 cup cooked chicken breast, sliced

- 1/2 cup sliced bell peppers
- 1/2 cup sliced red onions
- 1/2 cup sliced pineapple
- 2 tablespoons chopped green onions

Directions:

1. Preheat the oven.
2. Roll out the pizza dough on a floured surface to your desired thickness.
3. Transfer the rolled-out dough to a pizza stone or baking sheet.
4. Spread the teriyaki sauce evenly over the dough.
5. Sprinkle shredded mozzarella cheese over the sauce.
6. Arrange the cooked chicken, bell peppers, red onions, and pineapple on top of the cheese.
7. Bake in the preheated oven for about 12-15 minutes, or until the crust is golden and the cheese is melted and bubbly.

Nutritional Value (Amount per Serving):

Calories: 517; Fat: 18.55; Carb: 44.05; Protein: 42.98

Duck Confit Pizza

Prep Time: 20 Mins   Cook Time: 1 Hr 10 Mins   Serves: 4

Ingredients:

- 2 duck leg confits
- 1 pre-made pizza dough
- 1/2 cup tomato sauce
- 1 cup shredded mozzarella cheese
- 1/4 cup sliced black olives
- 1/4 cup sliced red bell pepper
- 1/4 cup sliced red onion
- Fresh thyme leaves, for garnish

Directions:

1. Preheat your oven to the temperature recommended on the pizza dough package.
2. Remove the skin from the duck confit and shred the meat.
3. Roll out the pizza dough on a floured surface to your desired thickness.
4. Transfer the dough to a baking sheet or pizza stone.
5. Spread the tomato sauce evenly over the dough.
6. Sprinkle the shredded duck confit, mozzarella cheese, black olives, red bell pepper, and red onion on top.
7. Bake in the preheated oven for the recommended time or until the crust is golden and the cheese is melted and bubbly.
8. Remove from the oven and garnish with fresh thyme leaves before serving.

Nutritional Value (Amount per Serving):

Calories: 265; Fat: 8.43; Carb: 21.78; Protein: 24.6

Chapter 6: Calzones and Sweet Hand Pizzas

Sweet Potato Pizza Crust

Prep Time: 15 Mins   Cook Time: 25 Mins   Serves: 8

Ingredients:

- 1 cup mashed sweet potato
- 3/4 cup white rice flour
- 1/3 cup tapioca flour
- 1 tsp baking powder
- 1/2 tsp salt
- cooking spray

Directions:

1. Peel and chop one medium sweet potato into chunks and boil it in a pot with water for about 10 minutes or until fork-tender. Discard the water and mash the sweet potato with a potato masher.
2. Mashed sweet potato in a black pot with a potato masher
3. Preheat oven. Add rice flour, tapioca flour, baking powder + salt, and mix with a spoon.
4. Once the mixture cooled down a little bit, use your hands to knead the pizza dough into a ball. If the dough is too dry, add a tiny bit of water or oil. If it's too sticky, add more rice flour.
5. Place the pizza dough onto a sheet of greased parchment paper and add a second sheet of parchment paper on top. Use a rolling pin to roll out the dough into your preferred shape.
6. Remove the top parchment paper and transfer the rolled-out pizza dough (including the bottom sheet of parchment paper) onto a baking sheet. Bake the pizza dough in the oven for about 10 minutes. Meanwhile, you can prepare your pizza toppings!
7. After 10 minutes, remove the pizza dough from the oven. Add the second parchment paper on top, and carefully flip the pizza dough over. Please don't burn your fingers! If the crust is too hot, simply wait a few minutes. Now, peel back the hot parchment paper.
8. Place your favorite toppings onto the sweet potato crust and return the pizza to the oven for about 10 to 18 minutes. If you just add a few toppings like vegan cheese and olives (for example) the pizza will be ready much faster than if you add lots of different veggies.

Nutritional Value (Amount per Serving):

Calories: 104; Fat: 2.14; Carb: 19.24; Protein: 1.6

Sweet Fruit Pizza

Prep Time: 25 Mins   Cook Time: 1 Hr 10 Mins   Serves: 6

Ingredients:

- 1 ¼ cups all-purpose flour
- 1 teaspoon cream of tartar

- ½ teaspoon baking soda
- ¼ teaspoon salt
- ½ cup butter, softened
- 1 ¼ cups white sugar, divided
- 1 large egg
- 1 (8 ounce) package cream cheese
- 2 teaspoons vanilla extract
- ½ cup fresh blueberries, or more to taste
- ½ cup sliced fresh strawberries, or more to taste
- ½ cup sliced banana, or more to taste

Directions:

1. Preheat the oven.
2. Make the cookie crust: Combine flour, cream of tartar, baking soda, and salt in a medium bowl and set aside. Cream together butter and 3/4 cup sugar until smooth in a large bowl. Add in egg and beat well. Stir dry ingredients into the creamed mixture until just blended.
3. Press dough into an ungreased pizza pan.
4. Bake in the preheated oven until lightly browned, 8 to 10 minutes. Cool.
5. Prepare the filling: Beat cream cheese with remaining 1/2 cup sugar and vanilla in a large bowl until light and fluffy. Spread evenly over the top of the cooled crust.
6. Arrange blueberries, strawberries, and banana on top of the filling, and chill.

Nutritional Value (Amount per Serving):

Calories: 507; Fat: 36.24; Carb: 39.83; Protein: 7.91

Strawberry Pizza

Prep Time: 15 Mins   Cook Time: 10 Mins   Serves: 8

Ingredients:

- 1 pre-made pizza dough
- 8 oz cream cheese, softened
- 1/2 cup powdered sugar
- 1 teaspoon vanilla extract
- 2 cups fresh strawberries, hulled and sliced
- 1/4 cup strawberry jam
- Fresh mint leaves, for garnish (optional)

Directions:

1. Preheat your oven.
2. Roll out the pizza dough on a lightly floured surface to your desired thickness.
3. Transfer the dough to a baking sheet or pizza stone.
4. In a bowl, mix the softened cream cheese, powdered sugar, and vanilla

extract until smooth.

5. Spread the cream cheese mixture evenly over the pizza dough.
6. Arrange the sliced strawberries on top of the cream cheese mixture.
7. In a small saucepan, heat the strawberry jam over low heat until melted and smooth.
8. Drizzle the melted strawberry jam over the strawberries.
9. Bake in the preheated oven for about 10-12 minutes, or until the crust is golden.
10. Remove from the oven and let it cool slightly before garnishing with fresh mint leaves, if desired.
11. Slice and serve.

Nutritional Value (Amount per Serving):

Calories: 157; Fat: 9.26; Carb: 15.69; Protein: 3.4

Blueberry Pizza

Prep Time: 10 Mins   Cook Time: 15 Mins   Serves: 4

Ingredients:

- 1 pre-made pizza crust
- 1 cup fresh blueberries
- 1/4 cup granulated sugar
- 1/4 teaspoon ground cinnamon
- 1/2 cup mascarpone cheese
- 1 tablespoon honey

Directions:

1. Preheat your oven to the temperature specified on the pizza crust package.
2. Place the pizza crust on a baking sheet.
3. In a small bowl, mix together the blueberries, sugar, and cinnamon.
4. Spread the mascarpone cheese evenly over the pizza crust.
5. Sprinkle the blueberry mixture over the cheese.
6. Drizzle the honey over the top.
7. Bake in the preheated oven according to the package instructions, or until the crust is golden brown and the blueberries are slightly softened.
8. Remove from the oven and let it cool for a few minutes before slicing and serving.

Nutritional Value (Amount per Serving):

Calories: 475; Fat: 21.47; Carb: 55.44; Protein: 16.47

Four Cheese Calzone

Prep Time: 15 Mins   Cook Time: 20 Mins   Serves: 4

Ingredients:

- 1 pound pizza dough
- 1/2 cup marinara sauce
- 1/4 cup shredded mozzarella cheese
- 1/4 cup shredded cheddar cheese
- 1/4 cup shredded provolone cheese
- 1/4 cup grated Parmesan cheese

Directions:

1. Preheat your oven.
2. Roll out the pizza dough into a large circle or rectangle, about 1/4 inch thick.
3. Spread the marinara sauce evenly over half of the dough, leaving a border around the edges.
4. Sprinkle the mozzarella cheese, cheddar cheese, provolone cheese, and Parmesan cheese evenly over the sauce.
5. Fold the other half of the dough over the toppings and pinch the edges to seal.
6. Transfer the calzone to a baking sheet and bake for 15-20 minutes, or until the crust is golden brown.
7. Remove from the oven and let it cool for a few minutes before slicing and serving.

Nutritional Value (Amount per Serving):

Calories: 413; Fat: 21.35; Carb: 35.95; Protein: 19.52

Peanut Butter Cup Dessert Pizza

Prep Time: 15 Mins   Cook Time: 10 Mins   Serves: 6

Ingredients:

- 1 (16.5 ounce) package refrigerated sugar cookie dough
- ⅓ cup softened butter
- 1 egg
- ½ cup confectioners' sugar
- 1 cup creamy peanut butter
- 15 miniature chocolate-covered peanut butter cups, halved
- 2 tablespoons chocolate chips

Directions:

1. Preheat oven.
2. Grease a pizza pan.
3. Mix cookie dough, softened butter, and egg together in a bowl.
4. Spread cookie dough mixture onto prepared pizza pan to cover entirely.
5. Bake in preheated oven until dough begins to brown, 10 to 12 minutes; set aside to cool.

6. Beat confectioners' sugar into peanut butter in a bowl until completely integrated.
7. Spread peanut butter mixture over cooled cookie dough crust.
8. Arrange halved peanut butter cups atop peanut butter layer.
9. Sprinkle chocolate chips around peanut butter cups.

Nutritional Value (Amount per Serving):

Calories: 863; Fat: 50.24; Carb: 91.21; Protein: 17.34

Spinach and Ricotta Pocket Pie

Prep Time: 25 Mins   Cook Time: 20 Mins   Serves: 4

Ingredients:

- 1 pound pizza dough
- 2 cups fresh spinach leaves
- 1 cup ricotta cheese
- 1/2 cup shredded mozzarella cheese
- 1/4 cup grated Parmesan cheese
- 1/4 teaspoon garlic powder
- Salt and pepper to taste
- 1 egg, beaten (for egg wash)

Directions:

1. Preheat your oven.
2. Divide the pizza dough into 4 equal portions.
3. Roll out each portion of dough into a circle or oval shape.
4. In a skillet, sauté the spinach leaves until wilted. Remove from heat and let it cool.
5. In a bowl, mix the ricotta cheese, shredded mozzarella cheese, grated Parmesan cheese, garlic powder, salt, and pepper.
6. Place a portion of the spinach mixture on one half of each dough portion.
7. Spoon a portion of the ricotta cheese mixture over the spinach.
8. Fold the other half of the dough over the fillings and press the edges to seal.
9. Use a fork to crimp the edges of the pocket pies.
10. Brush the tops of the pocket pies with beaten egg wash.
11. Place the pocket pies on a baking sheet and bake in the preheated oven for about 20-25 minutes, or until golden brown.
12. Remove from the oven and let them cool for a few minutes before serving.

Nutritional Value (Amount per Serving):

Calories: 531; Fat: 29.53; Carb: 37.59; Protein: 28.88

Pineapple Pizza

Prep Time: 15 Mins   Cook Time: 15 Mins   Serves: 4

Ingredients:

- 1 pre-made pizza crust
- 1/2 cup marinara sauce
- 1 cup shredded mozzarella cheese
- 1 cup diced pineapple
- 1/4 cup sliced ham
- 1/4 cup sliced red onion

Directions:

1. Preheat your oven to the temperature specified on the pizza crust package.
2. Place the pizza crust on a baking sheet.
3. Spread the marinara sauce evenly over the crust.
4. Sprinkle the mozzarella cheese over the sauce.
5. Arrange the diced pineapple, sliced ham, and sliced red onion over the cheese.
6. Bake in the preheated oven according to the package instructions, or until the crust is golden brown and the cheese is melted and bubbly.
7. Remove from the oven and let it cool for a few minutes before slicing and serving.

Nutritional Value (Amount per Serving):

Calories: 408; Fat: 16.43; Carb: 44.14; Protein: 22.04

Jam Pizza

Prep Time: 10 Mins   Cook Time: 15 Mins   Serves: 4

Ingredients:

- 1 pre-made pizza crust
- 1/2 cup fruit jam (your choice of flavor)
- 1/4 cup sliced almonds
- 1/4 cup shredded coconut
- Powdered sugar, for dusting

Directions:

1. Preheat your oven to the temperature specified on the pizza crust package.
2. Place the pizza crust on a baking sheet.
3. Spread the fruit jam evenly over the crust.
4. Sprinkle the sliced almonds and shredded coconut over the jam.
5. Bake in the preheated oven according to the package instructions, or until the crust is golden brown and the toppings are lightly toasted.
6. Remove from the oven and let it cool for a few minutes.
7. Dust with powdered sugar before serving.

Nutritional Value (Amount per Serving):

Calories: 439; Fat: 16.36; Carb: 60.62; Protein: 12.27

Simple Fruit Pizza

Prep Time: 20 Mins   Cook Time: 1 Hour 40 Mins   Serves: 6

Ingredients:

- 1 (18 ounce) package refrigerated sugar cookie dough
- 1 (8 ounce) package cream cheese, softened
- ⅓ cup white sugar
- ½ teaspoon vanilla extract
- 1 pint fresh strawberries, sliced
- 1 pint fresh blueberries
- 2 bananas, sliced
- 2 kiwis, peeled and sliced
- ½ cup orange marmalade
- 2 tablespoons water

Directions:

1. Preheat the oven. Lightly grease a pizza pan.
2. Press cookie dough into the prepared pizza pan; prick holes in dough with a fork.
3. Bake in the preheated oven until golden, 10 to 15 minutes. Allow cookie crust to cool.
4. Beat cream cheese, sugar, and vanilla extract in a bowl until smooth; spread over cooled crust. Arrange strawberries, blueberries, bananas, and kiwi decoratively over cream cheese mixture.
5. Mix orange marmalade and water in a small bowl; spoon mixture over fruit. Chill pizza for 1 hour before serving.

Nutritional Value (Amount per Serving):

Calories: 394; Fat: 15.04; Carb: 65.7; Protein: 5.34

Margherita Folded Calzone

Prep Time: 20 Mins   Cook Time: 20 Mins   Serves: 4

Ingredients:

- 1 pound pizza dough
- 1 cup shredded mozzarella cheese
- 2 tomatoes, sliced
- 1/4 cup fresh basil leaves
- 2 tablespoons olive oil
- Salt and pepper to taste
- 1 egg, beaten (for egg wash)
- Marinara sauce, for dipping (optional)

Directions:

1. Preheat your oven.

2. Divide the pizza dough into 4 equal portions.
3. Roll out each portion of dough into a circle or oval shape.
4. Place sliced tomatoes and fresh basil leaves on one half of each dough portion.
5. Drizzle olive oil over the tomatoes and basil.
6. Season with salt and pepper to taste.
7. Sprinkle shredded mozzarella cheese over the toppings.
8. Fold the other half of the dough over the toppings and press the edges to seal.
9. Use a fork to crimp the edges of the calzones.
10. Brush the tops of the calzones with beaten egg wash.
11. Place the calzones on a baking sheet and bake in the preheated oven for about 15-20 minutes, or until golden brown.
12. Remove from the oven and let them cool for a few minutes before serving. Serve with marinara sauce for dipping, if desired.

Nutritional Value (Amount per Serving):

Calories: 475; Fat: 26.44; Carb: 35.23; Protein: 24.27

Pizza Hut's sweet Hawaiian pizza

Prep Time: 45 Mins   Cook Time: 15 Mins   Serves: 8

Ingredients:

- 1 pre-made pizza dough
- ⅓ can tomato paste
- 1 tsp granulated sugar
- salt and ground black pepper, to taste
- ½ tbsp lemon juice
- ½ tsp Italian seasoning
- ¼ tsp garlic powder
- ¾ cup ham, cooked, sliced into cubes
- ¾ cup smoked bacon, chopped and cooked
- 1 cup pineapple chunks
- 2 cups mozzarella cheese, grated

Directions:

1. Preheat oven.
2. Combine the following Ingredients: tomato paste, sugar, salt, lemon juice, garlic powder, and Italian seasoning. Stir until well combined.
3. Spread the sauce over the pizza dough, then top with the meats, pineapple, and cheese.
4. Bake for 15 minutes, or until the cheese is melted and bubbly.
5. Slice and serve while warm.

Nutritional Value (Amount per Serving):

Calories: 153; Fat: 5.13; Carb: 16.14; Protein: 12.2

Fruit Pizza with White Chocolate

Prep Time: 20 Mins   Cook Time: 20 Mins   Serves: 8

Ingredients:

- ½ cup butter
- ½ cup shortening
- 1 ½ cups white sugar
- 2 eggs
- 2 ¾ cups all-purpose flour
- 2 teaspoons cream of tartar
- 1 teaspoon baking soda
- ¼ teaspoon salt
- 2 cups vanilla baking chips
- ¼ cup heavy cream
- 1 (8 ounce) package cream cheese
- 1 pint fresh strawberries, sliced
- ½ cup white sugar
- 2 tablespoons cornstarch
- 1 cup pineapple juice
- 1 teaspoon lemon juice

Directions:

1. Preheat oven. Lightly grease a cookie sheet.
2. For the crust: Cream together butter, shortening and 1 1/2 cups sugar with electric mixer. Beat in eggs. In a separate bowl, stir together flour, cream of tartar, baking soda and salt. Beat flour mixture into butter mixture to form a stiff dough. Press dough into a rectangle as large as the baking sheet.
3. Bake for 10 minutes in the preheated oven, or until light brown.
4. For the filling: In medium microwave safe bowl, microwave vanilla chips and cream on high 60 to 90 seconds, or until chips are melted and smooth after stirring. Beat in cream cheese with electric mixer until creamy. Spread on cooled cookie crust.
5. For the topping: Arrange sliced fruits decoratively over filling. In a medium saucepan over medium heat, combine 1/2 cup sugar, cornstarch, pineapple and lemon juices. Stir and cook until sugar dissolves and mixture thickens. Pour over fruits. Refrigerate until serving.

Nutritional Value (Amount per Serving):

Calories: 712; Fat: 49.45; Carb: 57.43; Protein: 12.22

Nuts Creamy Pizza

Prep Time: 15 Mins   Cook Time: 15 Mins   Serves: 4

Ingredients:

- 1 pre-made pizza crust
- 1/2 cup ricotta cheese
- 1/4 cup creamy peanut butter
- 2 tablespoons honey
- 1/4 cup chopped mixed nuts (such as almonds, walnuts, and cashews)
- 2 tablespoons chocolate chips (optional)

Directions:

1. Preheat your oven to the temperature specified on the pizza crust package.
2. Place the pizza crust on a baking sheet.
3. In a small bowl, mix together the ricotta cheese, peanut butter, and honey until well combined.
4. Spread the ricotta mixture evenly over the pizza crust.
5. Sprinkle the chopped mixed nuts and chocolate chips (if using) over the cheese.
6. Bake in the preheated oven according to the package instructions, or until the crust is golden brown and the cheese is melted.
7. Remove from the oven and let it cool for a few minutes before slicing and serving.

Nutritional Value (Amount per Serving):

Calories: 554; Fat: 27.91; Carb: 58.52; Protein: 18.74

Lemon Meringue Pizza

Prep Time: 20 Mins   Cook Time: 20 Mins   Serves: 8

Ingredients:

- 1 pre-made pizza dough
- 1 cup lemon curd
- 4 egg whites
- 1/2 cup granulated sugar
- 1/2 teaspoon vanilla extract
- Zest of 1 lemon

Directions:

1. Preheat your oven.
2. Roll out the pizza dough on a lightly floured surface to your desired thickness.
3. Transfer the dough to a baking sheet or pizza stone.
4. Spread the lemon curd evenly over the pizza dough.
5. In a clean mixing bowl, beat the egg whites until foamy.
6. Gradually add the granulated sugar while continuing to beat the egg whites.
7. Add the vanilla extract and lemon zest, and beat until stiff peaks form.
8. Spread the meringue mixture over the lemon curd, covering it completely.
9. Bake in the preheated oven for about 15-18 minutes, or until the meringue is golden.
10. Remove from the oven and let it cool for a few minutes before slicing and serving.

Nutritional Value (Amount per Serving):

Calories: 74; Fat: 1.11; Carb: 13.98; Protein: 2.8

Fruit Creamy Pizza

Prep Time: 15 Mins   Cook Time: 1 Hour 45 Mins   Serves: 4

Ingredients:

- 1 (16.5 ounce) package refrigerated sliceable sugar cookies, sliced
- 1 (8 ounce) package Cream Cheese, softened
- ¼ cup sugar
- ½ teaspoon vanilla
- 4 cups assorted cut-up fruit (kiwi, strawberries, blueberries, drained canned mandarin oranges)
- ¼ cup apricot preserves, pressed through sieve to remove lumps
- 1 tablespoon water

Directions:

1. Heat oven.
2. Line pizza pan with foil; spray with cooking spray. Arrange cookie dough slices in single layer in prepared pan; press together to form crust. Bake 14 min.; cool completely. Invert onto plate; carefully remove foil. Turn crust over.
3. Beat cream cheese, sugar and vanilla with mixer until well blended. Spread over crust.
4. Top with fruit. Mix preserves and water; brush over fruit. Refrigerate 2 hours.

Nutritional Value (Amount per Serving):

Calories: 804; Fat: 18.29; Carb: 165.57; Protein: 6.32

BBQ Chicken Stuffed Calzone

Prep Time: 25 Mins   Cook Time: 20 Mins   Serves: 4

Ingredients:

- 1 pound pizza dough
- 1 cup cooked chicken, shredded
- 1/2 cup BBQ sauce
- 1/2 cup shredded mozzarella cheese
- 1/4 cup red onion, thinly sliced
- 1/4 cup chopped fresh cilantro
- 1 egg, beaten (for egg wash)
- Ranch dressing, for dipping (optional)

Directions:

1. Preheat your oven.
2. Divide the pizza dough into 4 equal portions.
3. Roll out each portion of dough into a circle or oval shape.
4. In a bowl, mix the shredded chicken with BBQ sauce until well coated.

5. Place a portion of the BBQ chicken mixture on one half of each dough portion.
6. Sprinkle shredded mozzarella cheese, red onion, and chopped cilantro over the chicken.
7. Fold the other half of the dough over the toppings and press the edges to seal.
8. Use a fork to crimp the edges of the calzones.
9. Brush the tops of the calzones with beaten egg wash.
10. Place the calzones on a baking sheet and bake in the preheated oven for about 20-25 minutes, or until golden brown.
11. Remove from the oven and let them cool for a few minutes before serving. Serve with ranch dressing for dipping, if desired.

Nutritional Value (Amount per Serving):

Calories: 559; Fat: 34.45; Carb: 36.4; Protein: 25.83

Gluten Free Sweet Potato Pizza Crust

Prep Time: 5 Mins   Cook Time: 40 Mins   Serves: 8

Ingredients:

- 1 medium sweet potato, cooked and mashed
- 3/4 cup rolled oats
- 1/2 Tbsp Italian seasoning
- ¼ tsp garlic powder
- ¼ tsp paprika
- 2 Tbsp cornstarch
- Sea salt, for sprinkling

Directions:

1. Preheat oven. Add all ingredients to a high speed blender or food processor and process until very fine.
2. Transfer dough to a bowl to help mold into a ball (it may be sticky). Transfer and press dough onto a pizza pan coated with parchment paper. It's okay if the dough doesn't span the entirety of the pan.
3. Bake for 25-30 minutes.
4. Take out of oven and let cool. Once cooled, flip dough over, gently pulling parchment paper from what is now the top of pizza dough. Coat with olive oil and place back in the oven for 5-7 minutes, or until reaches desired crispiness.
5. Let cool and sprinkle with sea salt.

Nutritional Value (Amount per Serving):

Calories: 46; Fat: 0.66; Carb: 11.43; Protein: 1.84

Berry Pizza

Prep Time: 10 Mins   Cook Time: 40 Mins   Serves: 6

Ingredients:

- 1 cup all-purpose flour
- ½ cup confectioners' sugar
- ½ cup butter, melted
- 1 (8 ounce) package cream cheese, softened
- ½ cup white sugar
- 2 ½ cups strawberries, sliced
- ½ (2 ounce) package strawberry Danish dessert mix
- 1 cup water

Directions:

1. Preheat the oven.
2. In a medium bowl, mix together flour and confectioners' sugar. Stir in melted butter. Press mixture evenly into a pizza pan.
3. Bake in the preheated oven for 15 minutes. Allow to cool.
4. In a small mixing bowl, beat together cream cheese and white sugar until smooth. Spread over cooled crust. Arrange strawberries over cream cheese layer.
5. Combine custard mix and water in a small saucepan. Bring to a boil while stirring frequently. Boil and stir 1 minute. Pour mixture over strawberry layer. Chill before serving.

Nutritional Value (Amount per Serving):

Calories: 425; Fat: 30.38; Carb: 34.15; Protein: 6.04

Kids Favorite Passover Pizza

Prep Time: 10 Mins   Cook Time: 10 Mins   Serves: 4

Ingredients:

- ¼ cup spaghetti sauce
- 2 matzo crackers
- 1 pinch garlic salt
- 1 pinch dried oregano
- ¾ cup shredded mozzarella cheese
- 1 tomato, sliced
- ¼ cup sliced black olives

Directions:

1. Preheat oven.
2. Spread marinara sauce on the pieces of matzo. Sprinkle garlic salt and oregano over the tomato sauce. Cover with cheese, tomato slices, and olives. Place pizzas on cookie sheets.
3. Bake for 5 minutes, or until cheese has melted.

Nutritional Value (Amount per Serving):

Calories: 49; Fat: 0.69; Carb: 3.59; Protein: 7.16

Caramel Apple Crisp Pizza

Prep Time: 15 Mins   Cook Time: 30 Mins   Serves: 6

Ingredients:

- 1 pre-made pizza dough
- 2 medium-sized apples, peeled, cored, and thinly sliced
- 1/4 cup granulated sugar
- 1/4 cup all-purpose flour
- 1/4 cup rolled oats
- 1/4 cup brown sugar
- 1/2 teaspoon cinnamon
- 1/4 cup cold unsalted butter, cut into small pieces
- Caramel sauce, for drizzling

Directions:

1. Preheat your oven.
2. Roll out the pizza dough on a lightly floured surface to your desired thickness.
3. Transfer the dough to a baking sheet or pizza stone.
4. In a bowl, combine the granulated sugar, flour, rolled oats, brown sugar, and cinnamon.
5. Cut in the cold butter using a fork or pastry cutter until the mixture resembles coarse crumbs.
6. Arrange the sliced apples evenly over the pizza dough.
7. Sprinkle the crumb mixture over the apples, covering them completely.
8. Bake in the preheated oven for about 25-30 minutes, or until the crust is golden and the apples are tender.
9. Remove from the oven and let it cool for a few minutes.
10. Drizzle caramel sauce over the pizza before serving.

Nutritional Value (Amount per Serving):

Calories: 184; Fat: 6.91; Carb: 30.41; Protein: 2.9

Durian Pizza

Prep Time: 15 Mins   Cook Time: 15 Mins   Serves: 4

Ingredients:

- 1 pre-made pizza crust
- 1 cup durian flesh, mashed

- 1/4 cup condensed milk
- 1/4 cup shredded coconut
- 2 tablespoons chopped roasted peanuts

1. Preheat your oven to the temperature specified on the pizza crust package.
2. Place the pizza crust on a baking sheet.
3. Spread the mashed durian flesh evenly over the crust.
4. Drizzle the condensed milk over the durian.
5. Sprinkle the shredded coconut and chopped roasted peanuts over the top.
6. Bake in the preheated oven according to the package instructions, or until the crust is golden brown.
7. Remove from the oven and let it cool for a few minutes before slicing and serving.

Nutritional Value (Amount per Serving):

Calories: 465; Fat: 23.09; Carb: 51.46; Protein: 14.81

Sweet Corn Pizza

Prep Time: 25 Mins   Cook Time: 20 Mins   Serves: 4

Ingredients:

- 4 8-inches Italian bread shells (Boboli) or four 6 to 7-inch pita bread rounds
- ½ cup dried tomato pesto or basil pesto
- 1 14 ounce can artichoke hearts, drained and coarsely chopped
- 1 cup fresh corn kernels
- ½ cup chopped green sweet pepper
- 8 ounces fresh mozzarella cheese, cut into bite-size pieces; one 8-ounce package shredded
- 2 cups Italian-blend cheeses
- Fresh basil leaves

Directions:

1. Line a very large baking sheet (or two large baking sheets) with foil. Lightly coat foil with nonstick cooking spray. Place bread shells on prepared baking sheet. Bake in a 425°F oven for 5 minutes. Remove bread shells from oven.
2. Spread tomato pesto over bread shell, leaving a 1/2-inch border around the edges. Arrange artichoke hearts, corn and pepper on bread shell. Sprinkle with cheese. Bake for 12 to 15 minutes or until cheese is melted and pizzas are heated through. Sprinkle basil leaves over the tops of pizzas before serving.

Nutritional Value (Amount per Serving):

Calories: 998; Fat: 19.77; Carb: 150.07; Protein: 56.41

Buffalo Chicken Calzone

Prep Time: 20 Mins   Cook Time: 20 Mins   Serves: 4

Ingredients:

- 1 pound pizza dough
- 1/2 cup buffalo sauce
- 1/2 cup shredded cooked chicken
- 1/4 cup blue cheese crumbles
- 1/4 cup diced celery
- 1/4 cup diced red onion
- 1/4 cup shredded mozzarella cheese

Directions:

1. Preheat your oven.
2. Roll out the pizza dough into a large circle or rectangle, about 1/4 inch thick.
3. Spread the buffalo sauce evenly over half of the dough, leaving a border around the edges.
4. Sprinkle the shredded chicken, blue cheese crumbles, celery, red onion, and mozzarella cheese over the sauce.
5. Fold the other half of the dough over the toppings and pinch the edges to seal.
6. Transfer the calzone to a baking sheet and bake for 15-20 minutes, or until the crust is golden brown.
7. Remove from the oven and let it cool for a few minutes before slicing and serving.

Nutritional Value (Amount per Serving):

Calories: 452; Fat: 25.43; Carb: 35.82; Protein: 20.24

Blueberry Blast Pizza

Prep Time: 15 Mins   Cook Time: 10 Mins   Serves: 8

Ingredients:

- 1 pre-made pizza dough
- 1 cup fresh blueberries
- 1/4 cup granulated sugar
- 1 tablespoon cornstarch
- 1 tablespoon lemon juice
- 1/4 cup sliced almonds
- 1/4 cup blueberry jam

Directions:

1. Preheat your oven.
2. Roll out the pizza dough on a lightly floured surface to your desired thickness.
3. Transfer the dough to a baking sheet or pizza stone.
4. In a bowl, combine the blueberries, granulated sugar, cornstarch, and

lemon juice.

5. Spread the blueberry jam evenly over the pizza dough.
6. Spoon the blueberry mixture over the jam, spreading it out evenly.
7. Sprinkle the sliced almonds over the blueberries.
8. Bake in the preheated oven for about 10-12 minutes, or until the crust is golden and the blueberries are bubbling.
9. Remove from the oven and let it cool for a few minutes before serving.

Nutritional Value (Amount per Serving):

Calories: 85; Fat: 1.15; Carb: 18.07; Protein: 1.15

Chocolate Pizza

Prep Time: 10 Mins   Cook Time: 20 Mins   Serves: 6

Ingredients:

- 1 cup semisweet chocolate chips
- ½ cup shortening
- ½ cup all-purpose flour
- ½ cup white sugar
- 2 eggs
- 1 teaspoon baking powder
- ¾ cup semisweet chocolate chips
- 2 tablespoons shortening
- 2 tablespoons water

Directions:

1. Melt 1 cup chocolate chips, and 1/2 cup shortening in a double boiler; cool. Stir in flour, sugar, eggs, and baking powder with fork. Spread crust evenly onto a well greased pizza pan.
2. Bake for 15 minutes. Cool.
3. Combine 3/4 cup chocolate chips, 2 tablespoons shortening, and water. Melt in a double boiler. Stir until smooth. Spread glaze evenly over cooled chocolate crust. Decorate as desired with candies.

Nutritional Value (Amount per Serving):

Calories: 735; Fat: 51.71; Carb: 62.96; Protein: 8.66

Chapter 7: Beyond Pizza

Beyond Meat and Mushroom Pizza

Prep Time: 10 Mins   Cook Time: 20 Mins   Serves: 4

Ingredients:

- 1 sheet of ready-made pizza dough
- 2 tablespoons of olive oil
- 1/4 cup of chopped mushrooms
- 1/4 cup of chopped onion
- 2 cloves of garlic
- salt and pepper to taste
- 1/4 cup of grated cheese
- 1/4 cup of Vegan Meat crumbles

Directions:

1. Preheat oven.
2. Brush the pizza dough with olive oil and spread the Vegan Meat crumbles evenly over it. Sprinkle the cheese on top and bake for 15 minutes or until golden and bubbly. In a skillet over medium-high heat, cook the mushrooms and onion with garlic, salt and pepper until soft and browned.
3. Spread the mushroom mixture over the cheese layer and return to the oven for another 5 minutes or until the cheese is melted. Cut into slices and enjoy!

Nutritional Value (Amount per Serving):

Calories: 166; Fat: 10.59; Carb: 11.96; Protein: 6.56

Beyond Veggie Lovers Pizza

Prep Time: 25 Mins   Cook Time: 20 Mins   Serves: 4

Ingredients:

- 1 pre-made pizza crust
- 1/2 cup pizza sauce
- 1 cup shredded vegan cheese
- 1/2 cup sliced bell peppers
- 1/2 cup sliced mushrooms
- 1/2 cup sliced black olives
- 1/4 cup sliced red onions
- 1/4 cup chopped fresh spinach
- Fresh basil leaves, for garnish

Directions:

1. Preheat your oven to the temperature specified on the pizza crust package.
2. Place the pizza crust on a baking sheet.
3. Spread the pizza sauce evenly over the crust.
4. Sprinkle the shredded vegan cheese over the sauce.
5. Arrange the sliced bell peppers, mushrooms, black olives, red onions, and chopped spinach over the cheese.
6. Bake in the preheated oven according to the package instructions, or until the crust is golden brown and the cheese is melted and bubbly.
7. Remove from the oven and let it cool for a few minutes.

8.Garnish with fresh basil leaves before serving.

Nutritional Value (Amount per Serving):

Calories: 482; Fat: 28.44; Carb: 35.81; Protein: 21.17

Beyond Beef Burger Pizza

Prep Time: 60 Mins   Cook Time: 15 Mins   Serves: 4

Ingredients:

- 1 lb store bought pizza dough, split in half
- 1 cup plant-based mixed shredded mozzarella and cheddar cheese
- ¼ red onion, diced
- ½ lb Beyond Beef
- 4 tbsp olive oil
- 2 cloves garlic, minced
- ½ medium tomato, diced (roughly ½ cup diced tomato)
- ½ cup pickle coins
- ¼ red onion, sliced
- ¼ cup plant-based Thousand Island

Directions:

1.An hour prior to cooking the pizza, preheat your oven with a pizza stone or cast-iron on the center rack. Remove your dough from the fridge and cut it in half. Use your fingers to push the edges of the dough underneath itself to form each half into a dough ball. Place the two dough balls on a floured surface covered with a damp cloth and let it come to room temperature.

2.While the oven is preheating, heat up 1 tbsp olive oil over medium heat. Add the chopped onion and let cook for 2 minutes. Add ½ lb Beyond Beef and break into crumbles with a wooden spoon. Season with salt and pepper and cook for 5-6 minutes until browned.

3.After the hour is up, use the tips of your fingers to press each dough ball into a disc then stretch or toss the dough until it has spread into a circle of roughly 9-10 inch diameter.

4.To assemble each pizza place the dough on a well-floured surface and drizzle with 1 ½ tbsp olive oil and 1 clove minced garlic. Use your fingers or a pastry brush to evenly spread the garlic and olive oil. Then top each pizza with ½ cup plant-based cheese, ½ the ground beef mixture, ¼ cup tomatoes, ¼ cup pickles, and ½ the red onion.

5.Remove the hot pizza stone or cast-iron from the oven and carefully slide your pizza onto the preheated pan. Return the stone/cast-iron into the oven and let cook for about 4-5 minutes until the crust has puffed up. Bake for an additional 2-3 minutes until the crust is browned.

6. Remove the pizza from the oven, cut and drizzle with plant-based Thousand Island to serve. Repeat with the second pizza.

Calories: 354; Fat: 23.82; Carb: 18.49; Protein: 17.28

Beyond Buffalo Chicken Pizza

Prep Time: 20 Mins   Cook Time: 20 Mins   Serves: 4

Ingredients:

- 1 pre-made pizza dough
- 1/2 cup buffalo sauce
- 1 cup shredded mozzarella cheese
- 1 cup cooked vegan chicken strips, diced
- 1/4 cup sliced red onions
- 2 tablespoons chopped fresh cilantro
- Ranch or blue cheese dressing for drizzling (optional)

Directions:

1. Preheat your oven to the temperature indicated on the pizza dough package.
2. Roll out the pizza dough on a lightly floured surface to your desired thickness.
3. Transfer the dough to a pizza stone or baking sheet.
4. Spread the buffalo sauce evenly over the dough, leaving a small border around the edges.
5. Sprinkle the shredded mozzarella cheese over the sauce.
6. Top with diced vegan chicken strips and sliced red onions.
7. Bake in the preheated oven for the time specified on the pizza dough package or until the crust is golden and the cheese is melted and slightly browned.
8. Remove from the oven and sprinkle with chopped fresh cilantro.
9. Drizzle with ranch or blue cheese dressing if desired.
10. Allow it to cool for a few minutes, then slice and serve.

Nutritional Value (Amount per Serving):

Calories: 193; Fat: 4.95; Carb: 14.19; Protein: 22.36

Spicy Beyond Meat Pizza

Prep Time: 15 Mins   Cook Time: 20 Mins   Serves: 4

Ingredients:

- 1 pre-made pizza dough
- 1/2 cup pizza sauce

- 1 package Vegan Meat, crumbled
- 1 jalapeno pepper, thinly sliced
- 1/2 red onion, thinly sliced
- 1 cup sliced mushrooms
- 1 cup shredded vegan pepper jack cheese
- Crushed red pepper flakes for garnish (optional)

Directions:

1. Preheat your oven to the temperature recommended on the pizza dough package.
2. Roll out the pizza dough on a floured surface and transfer it to a greased baking sheet.
3. Spread the pizza sauce evenly over the dough, leaving a small border around the edges.
4. Sprinkle the crumbled Vegan Meat over the sauce, followed by the jalapeno pepper, red onion, and mushrooms.
5. Top with vegan pepper jack cheese.
6. Bake in the preheated oven according to the pizza dough package instructions or until the crust is golden and the cheese is melted and bubbly.
7. Remove from the oven, garnish with crushed red pepper flakes if desired, let it cool for a few minutes, then slice and serve.

Nutritional Value (Amount per Serving):

Calories: 244; Fat: 14.38; Carb: 18.22; Protein: 11.05

Beyond Italian Style Sausage Supreme Pizza

Prep Time: 10 Mins   Cook Time: 15 Mins   Serves: 4

Ingredients:

- 1 package Vegan Sweet Italian Sausage, sliced
- 4 cups thinly sliced bell pepper
- 2 cups thinly sliced red onion
- 1-2 jalapeño pepper, thinly sliced
- 2 garlic cloves, minced
- 4 small balls of pizza dough
- 8 oz plant-based shredded mozzarella
- 8 oz plant-based fresh mozzarella
- 1 tbsp chopped oregano
- All-purpose flour
- Olive oil
- Salt

Directions:

1. Preheat your oven to the temperature specified on your pizza dough package.
2. Lightly grease a baking sheet with olive oil.
3. Shape the pizza dough to your desired size on the baking sheet.
4. Spread a thin layer of pizza sauce evenly over the dough.
5. Add the Vegan Sweet Italian Sausage slices, thinly sliced bell pepper, thinly

sliced red onion, and thinly sliced jalapeño pepper.

6. Sprinkle with plant-based shredded mozzarella and plant-based fresh mozzarella.
7. Bake for about 15 minutes or until the crust is golden brown and the cheese is melted.

Calories: 866; Fat: 36.17; Carb: 71.1; Protein: 63.86

Beyond Meat BBQ Ranch Pizza

Prep Time: 15 Mins   Cook Time: 15 Mins   Serves: 4

Ingredients:

- 1 pre-made pizza dough
- 1/4 cup ranch dressing
- 1/4 cup BBQ sauce
- 1 package Vegan Meat, crumbled
- 1/2 red onion, thinly sliced
- 1 cup shredded vegan cheddar cheese
- Fresh cilantro for garnish (optional)

Directions:

1. Preheat your oven.
2. Roll out the pizza dough on a floured surface and transfer it to a greased baking sheet.
3. In a small bowl, mix together the ranch dressing and BBQ sauce. Spread this mixture evenly over the dough, leaving a small border around the edges.
4. Sprinkle the crumbled Vegan Meat over the sauce, followed by the red onion.
5. Top with vegan cheddar cheese.
6. Bake in the preheated oven according to the pizza dough package instructions or until the crust is golden and the cheese is melted and bubbly.

Nutritional Value (Amount per Serving):

Calories: 176; Fat: 11.16; Carb: 16.47; Protein: 3.14

Beyond Veggie Supreme Pizza

Prep Time: 20 Mins   Cook Time: 15 Mins   Serves: 4

Ingredients:

- 1 pre-made pizza dough
- 1/2 cup pizza sauce
- 1 cup shredded mozzarella cheese
- 1/4 cup sliced red onions
- 1/4 cup sliced bell peppers
- 1/4 cup sliced mushrooms
- 1/4 cup sliced black olives
- 1/4 cup sliced zucchini
- Fresh basil leaves for garnish

Directions:

1. Preheat your oven to the temperature indicated on the pizza dough package.
2. Roll out the pizza dough on a lightly floured surface to your desired thickness.
3. Transfer the dough to a pizza stone or baking sheet.
4. Spread the pizza sauce evenly over the dough, leaving a small border around the edges.
5. Sprinkle the shredded mozzarella cheese over the sauce.
6. Arrange the sliced red onions, bell peppers, mushrooms, black olives, and zucchini on top.
7. Bake in the preheated oven for the time specified on the pizza dough package or until the crust is golden and the cheese is melted and slightly browned.
8. Remove from the oven and garnish with fresh basil leaves.
9. Allow it to cool for a few minutes, then slice and serve.

Nutritional Value (Amount per Serving):

Calories: 136; Fat: 3.27; Carb: 15.36; Protein: 11.63

Beyond Sausage Poblano Queso With Banza Pizza Crust Chips

Prep Time: 10 Mins   Cook Time: 20 Mins   Serves: 6-8

Ingredients:

- 2 links Hot Italian vegan sausage
- 1 box Banza pizza crusts (2 crusts)
- 2 cups raw cashews
- 1 small poblano pepper (about ⅓cup), seeds removed & finely chopped
- 2 cloves garlic
- ¼ cup nutritional yeast
- 2 tsp chili powder
- 2 tsp ground cumin, divided
- 2 tbsp harissa
- Salsa, hot sauce, or fresh cilantro leaves for garnish

Directions:

1. Preheat oven. Place cashews in a medium bowl with 1 ½ cups hot water and set aside to soak. Remove Banza pizza crusts from freezer to thaw slightly at room temperature.
2. Heat 1 tbsp olive oil in a large non-stick skillet over medium-high heat. When oil is shimmering, add finely chopped poblano. Cook until soft, about 5 minutes.
3. Remove the outer Vegan Sausage casing. Add Beyond Sausage to pan with the peppers. Continue to cook, breaking the sausage into small crumbles about 6-8 minutes, until crisp. Remove from heat and set aside.
4. In a blender or food processor, combine soaked cashews and water, garlic cloves, nutritional yeast, chili powder, half of cumin (1 tsp), harissa and 1 tsp salt. Blend until smooth (tip: we recommend using a high speed blender, as this will give you the creamiest, smoothest queso!).
5. Add more water as needed until desired consistency is reached. To kick up the heat, add some cayenne to the blender or finish with a drizzle of hot sauce. If the dip becomes too thin, add a few more cashews. Taste and adjust seasonings as desired.
6. Cut Banza pizza crust into triangles or strips. In a large bowl, gently toss the crust with 1 tbsp olive oil, remaining cumin (1 tsp) and ½ tsp salt until coated.
7. Bake the crust for 5-8 minutes, or until golden and crisp. Alternatively, place seasoned crust on a baking sheet and bake for 10-12 minutes.
8. Pour dip into a serving bowl. Stir in Beyond Meat sausage and poblanos. Garnish with a spoon of salsa, a drizzle of hot sauce or fresh cilantro. Serve with seasoned Banza pizza crust chips for dipping. Enjoy!

Nutritional Value (Amount per Serving):

Calories: 690; Fat: 50.46; Carb: 43.75; Protein: 22.48

Beyond Meat Supreme Pizza

Prep Time: 15 Mins   Cook Time: 20 Mins   Serves: 4

Ingredients:

- 1 pre-made pizza dough
- 1/2 cup pizza sauce
- 1 package Vegan Meat, crumbled
- 1/2 green bell pepper, sliced
- 1/2 red onion, sliced
- 1/2 cup sliced black olives
- 1 cup shredded vegan mozzarella cheese

- 1 teaspoon dried oregano
- Salt and pepper to taste

1. Preheat your oven to the temperature recommended on the pizza dough package.
2. Roll out the pizza dough on a floured surface and transfer it to a greased baking sheet.
3. Spread the pizza sauce evenly over the dough, leaving a small border around the edges.
4. Sprinkle the crumbled Vegan Meat over the sauce, followed by the bell pepper, red onion, and black olives.
5. Top with vegan mozzarella cheese, dried oregano, salt, and pepper.
6. Bake in the preheated oven according to the pizza dough package instructions or until the crust is golden and the cheese is melted and bubbly.
7. Remove from the oven, let it cool for a few minutes, then slice and serve.

Nutritional Value (Amount per Serving):

Calories: 156; Fat: 4.57; Carb: 17.47; Protein: 11.94

Beyond Sausage Pizza With Pesto Cream and Cauliflower Crust

Prep Time: 15 Mins   Cook Time: 15 Mins   Serves: 4

Ingredients:

- esto Cream:
- 1 cup Anchor Shelf Stable Cooking Cream
- 4 Tbsp. Arrezzio basil pesto
- Salt and freshly ground black pepper to taste
- eyond Sausage Pizza:
- 1 Sysco Simply Cauliflower Pizza Crust
- ¼ lb. Arrezzio Imperial fresh mozzarella, sliced into ¼-inch rounds
- 1 Vegan Sausage, cooked and sliced into 1/8-inch rounds
- 6 broccolini stalks, trimmed to 2-3 inches, blanched and shocked
- 3 oz. Peppadew red peppers
- 1 Tbsp. Arrezzio Imperial olive oil

Directions:

For Pesto Cream
1. In a small sauté pan over medium heat, thicken the Anchor cream by half.
2. Once thickened, whisk in the basil pesto. Season with salt and pepper and

set aside to chill.

For The Pizza

1. Place the cauliflower crust on a sheet pan or pizza screen. Spread the pesto cream evenly over the crust, leaving a half-inch border around the outside.
2. Arrange the mozzarella, sausage, broccolini and peppers evenly around the crust.
3. Brush the outer edge of the crust with the olive oil.
4. Bake in a convection oven until the cheese has melted and the crust is browned.

Nutritional Value (Amount per Serving):

Calories: 1132; Fat: 58.39; Carb: 92.01; Protein: 62.2

Beyond Mediterranean Pizza

Prep Time: 20 Mins   Cook Time: 15 Mins   Serves: 4

Ingredients:

- 1 pre-made pizza dough
- 1/4 cup olive oil
- 2 cloves garlic, minced
- 1/2 cup crumbled feta cheese
- 1/4 cup sliced Kalamata olives
- 1/4 cup sliced sun-dried tomatoes
- 1/4 cup chopped artichoke hearts
- 2 tablespoons chopped fresh basil

Directions:

1. Preheat your oven to the temperature indicated on the pizza dough package.
2. Roll out the pizza dough on a lightly floured surface to your desired thickness.
3. In a small bowl, mix together the olive oil and minced garlic.
4. Brush the garlic-infused olive oil over the pizza dough.
5. Sprinkle the crumbled feta cheese evenly over the dough.
6. Top with sliced Kalamata olives, sun-dried tomatoes, and chopped artichoke hearts.
7. Bake in the preheated oven for the time specified on the pizza dough package or until the crust is golden and the cheese is slightly melted.
8. Remove from the oven and sprinkle with fresh basil.
9. Allow it to cool for a few minutes, then slice and serve.

Nutritional Value (Amount per Serving):

Calories: 260; Fat: 20.51; Carb: 14.91; Protein: 5.43

BBQ Beyond Meat Delight

Prep Time: 20 Mins   Cook Time: 20 Mins   Serves: 4

Ingredients:

- 1 pre-made pizza crust
- 1/2 cup BBQ sauce
- 1 cup shredded vegan cheese
- 1/2 cup sliced red onions
- 1/4 cup chopped fresh cilantro
- 1/2 cup crumbled Beyond Meat (plant-based meat substitute)
- 1/4 cup sliced jalapenos (optional)

Directions:

1. Preheat your oven to the temperature specified on the pizza crust package.
2. Place the pizza crust on a baking sheet.
3. Spread the BBQ sauce evenly over the crust.
4. Sprinkle the shredded vegan cheese over the sauce.
5. Arrange the sliced red onions, chopped cilantro, crumbled Beyond Meat, and sliced jalapenos (if using) over the cheese.
6. Bake in the preheated oven according to the package instructions, or until the crust is golden brown and the cheese is melted and bubbly.
7. Remove from the oven and let it cool for a few minutes before slicing and serving.

Nutritional Value (Amount per Serving):

Calories: 491; Fat: 26.68; Carb: 38.87; Protein: 25

Beyond Hawaiian Pizza

Prep Time: 15 Mins   Cook Time: 15 Mins   Serves: 4

Ingredients:

- 1 pre-made pizza dough
- 1/2 cup pizza sauce
- 1 cup shredded mozzarella cheese
- 1/2 cup diced pineapple
- 1/4 cup sliced red onions
- 1/4 cup diced Vegan ham
- Fresh cilantro (optional)

Directions:

1. Preheat your oven to the temperature indicated on the pizza dough package.
2. Roll out the pizza dough on a lightly floured surface to your desired thickness.
3. Transfer the dough to a pizza stone or baking sheet.
4. Spread the pizza sauce evenly over the dough, leaving a small border around the edges.
5. Sprinkle the shredded mozzarella cheese over the sauce.
6. Top with diced pineapple, sliced red onions, and diced Vegan ham.

7. Bake in the preheated oven for the time specified on the pizza dough package, or until the crust is golden and the cheese is bubbly.
8. Remove from the oven and let it cool for a few minutes.
9. Garnish with fresh cilantro if desired, then slice and serve.

Nutritional Value (Amount per Serving):

Calories: 146; Fat: 2.44; Carb: 19.45; Protein: 11.85

Beyond Pesto and Tomato Pizza

Prep Time: 15 Mins   Cook Time: 15 Mins   Serves: 4

Ingredients:

- 1 pre-made pizza dough
- 1/2 cup basil pesto
- 1 cup shredded mozzarella cheese
- 1 cup cherry tomatoes, halved
- 1/4 cup sliced red onions
- Fresh basil leaves for garnish

Directions:

1. Preheat your oven to the temperature indicated on the pizza dough package.
2. Roll out the pizza dough on a lightly floured surface to your desired thickness.
3. Transfer the dough to a pizza stone or baking sheet.
4. Spread the basil pesto evenly over the dough, leaving a small border around the edges.
5. Sprinkle the shredded mozzarella cheese over the pesto.
6. Arrange the halved cherry tomatoes and sliced red onions on top.
7. Bake in the preheated oven for the time specified on the pizza dough package or until the crust is golden and the cheese is melted and slightly browned.
8. Remove from the oven and garnish with fresh basil leaves.
9. Allow it to cool for a few minutes, then slice and serve.

Nutritional Value (Amount per Serving):

Calories: 131; Fat: 2.08; Carb: 17.34; Protein: 11.35

Beyond Meat Buffalo Chicken Pizza

Prep Time: 15 Mins   Cook Time: 15 Mins   Serves: 4

Ingredients:

- 1 pre-made pizza dough
- 1/4 cup vegan buffalo sauce
- 1 package Vegan Meat, crumbled

- 1/2 cup sliced red onion
- 1/2 cup sliced bell peppers
- 1 cup shredded vegan mozzarella cheese
- Vegan ranch dressing for drizzling (optional)

Directions:

1. Preheat your oven to the temperature recommended on the pizza dough package.
2. Roll out the pizza dough on a floured surface and transfer it to a greased baking sheet.
3. Spread the vegan buffalo sauce evenly over the dough, leaving a small border around the edges.
4. Sprinkle the crumbled Vegan Meat over the sauce, followed by the red onion and bell peppers.
5. Top with vegan mozzarella cheese.
6. Bake in the preheated oven according to the pizza dough package instructions or until the crust is golden and the cheese is melted and bubbly.
7. Remove from the oven, drizzle with vegan ranch dressing if desired, let it cool for a few minutes, then slice and serve.

Nutritional Value (Amount per Serving):

Calories: 182; Fat: 5.85; Carb: 21.41; Protein: 11.26

Beyond Pizza Rolls

Prep Time: 10 Mins   Cook Time: 20 Mins   Serves: 2-4

Ingredients:

- 1 pack of Beyond Sausage Hot Italian
- 13 oz pizza sauce
- 8 oz plant-based mozzarella
- 1 Tbs pizza seasoning (or Italian)
- Phyllo dough
- ¼ cup melted plant-based butter or olive oil
- Parsley to top

Directions:

1. Crumble Beyond Sausage into a pan on medium-high heat. Cook according to package instructions until crumbles begin turning brown.
2. Add in all of the pizza sauce, plant based cheese, and pizza seasoning, and stir as it cooks until the cheese is melted and warm. This will be your pizza pocket filling.
3. Lay out 1 sheet of phyllo dough on a clean surface, lighting brushing with

melted plant based butter or olive oil.

4. Layer another sheet on top of that.

5. Cut your double-layer sheet into quarters, slicing down the center horizontally and vertically.

6. With your rectangle chunk in front of you, oriented so the long side is vertical, take each rectangle and place 1-2 Tablespoons of filling 1 inch from the top of the rectangle in the center. Fold over the left side on top of the filling, then the right side, tri-folding the rectangle so you end up with a skinny rectangle. Fold the filling chunk downward into small square sections. (Alternatively, fold the phyllo dough the way you prefer to get a small 'pocket')

7. Repeat with all of the rectangles, creating new ones with sheets of phyllo dough until all of the filling has been used.

8. Spray or lightly coat 'pockets' with oil or butter.

9. Bake for about 7-10 minutes until crispy.

10. Top with parsley and serve with marinara and/or ranch.

Nutritional Value (Amount per Serving):

Calories: 835; Fat: 43.92; Carb: 20.38; Protein: 89.57

Beyond Sausage and Peppers Pizza

Prep Time: 20 Mins   Cook Time: 20 Mins   Serves: 4

Ingredients:

- 1 pre-made pizza dough
- 1/2 cup pizza sauce
- 1/2 cup shredded mozzarella cheese
- 4 Vegan Sausage links, sliced
- 1 bell pepper, thinly sliced
- 1/2 red onion, thinly sliced
- 1/4 cup sliced black olives
- 1/4 teaspoon dried oregano
- 1/4 teaspoon dried basil
- Salt and pepper, to taste

Directions:

1. Preheat your oven to the temperature specified on the pizza dough package.

2. Roll out the pizza dough on a floured surface to your desired thickness.

3. Transfer the dough to a pizza stone or baking sheet.

4. Spread the pizza sauce evenly over the dough.

5. Sprinkle the shredded mozzarella cheese over the sauce.

6. Arrange the sliced Vegan Sausage, bell pepper, red onion, and black olives on top.

7. Sprinkle the dried oregano, dried basil, salt, and pepper over the toppings.

8. Bake in the preheated oven for the time specified on the pizza dough package, or until the crust is golden and the cheese is melted and bubbly.

9. Remove from the oven, slice, and serve.

Nutritional Value (Amount per Serving):

Calories: 247; Fat: 10.39; Carb: 18.02; Protein: 20.95

Beyond Meat Pesto Veggie Pizza

Prep Time: 15 Mins   Cook Time: 15 Mins   Serves: 4

Ingredients:

- 1 pre-made pizza dough
- 1/4 cup vegan pesto sauce
- 1 package Vegan Meat, crumbled
- 1/2 cup sliced cherry tomatoes
- 1/2 cup sliced mushrooms
- 1/2 cup sliced black olives
- 1 cup shredded vegan mozzarella cheese
- Fresh basil leaves for garnish

Directions:

1. Preheat your oven to the temperature recommended on the pizza dough package.
2. Roll out the pizza dough on a floured surface and transfer it to a greased baking sheet.
3. Spread the vegan pesto sauce evenly over the dough, leaving a small border around the edges.
4. Sprinkle the crumbled Vegan Meat over the sauce, followed by the cherry tomatoes, mushrooms, and black olives.
5. Top with vegan mozzarella cheese.
6. Bake in the preheated oven according to the pizza dough package instructions or until the crust is golden and the cheese is melted and bubbly.
7. Remove from the oven, garnish with fresh basil leaves, let it cool for a few minutes, then slice and serve.

Nutritional Value (Amount per Serving):

Calories: 251; Fat: 14.32; Carb: 19.24; Protein: 12.84

Beyond Meat-free Pizza

Prep Time: 15 Mins   Cook Time: 20 Mins   Serves: 4

Ingredients:

- 1 pre-made pizza crust
- 1/2 cup pizza sauce
- 1 cup shredded vegan cheese
- 1/2 cup sliced bell peppers
- 1/2 cup sliced red onions
- 1/4 cup sliced black olives
- Fresh basil leaves, for garnish

1. Preheat your oven to the temperature specified on the pizza crust package.
2. Place the pizza crust on a baking sheet.
3. Spread the pizza sauce evenly over the crust.
4. Sprinkle the shredded vegan cheese over the sauce.
5. Arrange the sliced bell peppers, red onions, and black olives over the cheese.
6. Bake in the preheated oven according to the package instructions, or until the crust is golden brown and the cheese is melted and bubbly.
7. Remove from the oven and let it cool for a few minutes.
8. Garnish with fresh basil leaves before serving.

Nutritional Value (Amount per Serving):

Calories: 475; Fat: 27.54; Carb: 35.86; Protein: 21.1

Beyond Beef Nachos

Prep Time: 5 Mins   Cook Time: 15 Mins   Serves: 6-8

Ingredients:

- 16 oz (1 package) Vegan Beef
- 1 tbsp extra virgin olive oil
- 1 medium yellow onion, diced
- 1 tbsp taco seasoning
- 1 tbsp cumin
- 1 tbsp lime juice
- 1 tsp lime zest
- 1 large bag tortilla chips
- 1 large tomato diced
- ¼ cup green onion
- ¼ cup cilantro
- 1 jalapeño thinly sliced, de-seeded
- 1 cup queso
- Pinch of salt, to taste
- Pinch of pepper, to taste

Directions:

1. Preheat oven.
2. Warm oil in a large pan, add onion and cook for a minute. Add Vegan Beef and cook for 2 minutes. Add taco seasoning, cumin, lime juice and lime zest. Cook for about four more minutes.
3. In a large baking dish, place tortilla chips and layer in beef. Add cheese. Bake for 10 minutes or so until chips are golden and crispy.
4. Garnish with tomato, green onion, cilantro, jalapeño, salt and pepper. Dig in!

Nutritional Value (Amount per Serving):

Calories: 315; Fat: 12.19; Carb: 31.19; Protein: 21.45

Beyond Meat and Spinach Pizza

Prep Time: 10 Mins   Cook Time: 20 Mins   Serves: 4

Ingredients:

- 1 sheet of ready-made pizza dough
- 2 tablespoons of olive oil
- 1/4 cup of chopped spinach leaves
- 1/4 cup of chopped cherry tomatoes
- 2 cloves of garlic, salt and pepper to taste
- 1/4 cup of grated cheese
- 1/4 cup of Vegan Meat crumbles

Directions:

1. Preheat oven.
2. Brush the pizza dough with olive oil and spread the Vegan Meat crumbles evenly over it. Sprinkle the cheese on top and bake for 15 minutes or until golden and bubbly.
3. In a small bowl, toss the spinach leaves with cherry tomatoes, garlic, salt and pepper.
4. Spread the spinach mixture over the cheese layer and return to the oven for another 5 minutes or until the cheese is melted.

Nutritional Value (Amount per Serving):

Calories: 121; Fat: 9.57; Carb: 4.95; Protein: 4.6

Beyond Meat Loaded Pizza

Prep Time: 10 Mins   Cook Time: 20 Mins   Serves: 4

Ingredients:

- 1 Package Vegan Sausage
- 1 Package Vegan Burger
- Vegan Pizza Dough
- 4 Cups Vegan Mozzarella Cheese
- 1 White Onion
- 1 Red Bell pepper
- 2 Cups Marinara Sauce
- 2 TBSP Pitted Olives
- 1 Cup Shittake Mushrooms
- ½ Cup Roughly Chopped Basil
- Avocado Oil

Directions:

1. Preheat your oven.
1. Lightly grease a baking sheet with avocado oil.
2. Shape the pizza dough to your desired size on the baking sheet.
3. Spread a thin layer of marinara sauce evenly over the dough.
4. Cook the Vegan Sausage and Vegan Burger in a pan until browned, then add them to the pizza.
5. Add thinly sliced white onion and red bell pepper.
6. Add shiitake mushrooms and pitted olives.

7. Sprinkle with vegan mozzarella cheese.
8. Bake for about 15-20 minutes or until the crust is golden brown and the cheese is melted.
9. Garnish with roughly chopped basil before serving.

Nutritional Value (Amount per Serving):

Calories: 367; Fat: 8.58; Carb: 30.63; Protein: 44.86

Beyond BBQ Vegetable Pizza

Prep Time: 20 Mins   Cook Time: 20 Mins   Serves: 4

Ingredients:

- 1 pre-made pizza dough
- 1/2 cup BBQ sauce
- 1 cup shredded mozzarella cheese
- 1/4 cup sliced red onions
- 1/4 cup sliced bell peppers
- 1/4 cup sliced zucchini
- 1/4 cup sliced corn kernels
- 1/4 cup chopped fresh cilantro

Directions:

1. Preheat your oven to the temperature indicated on the pizza dough package.
2. Roll out the pizza dough on a lightly floured surface to your desired thickness.
3. Transfer the dough to a pizza stone or baking sheet.
4. Spread the BBQ sauce evenly over the dough, leaving a small border around the edges.
5. Sprinkle the shredded mozzarella cheese over the sauce.
6. Arrange the sliced red onions, bell peppers, zucchini, and corn kernels on top.
7. Bake in the preheated oven for the time specified on the pizza dough package or until the crust is golden and the cheese is melted and slightly browned.
8. Remove from the oven and sprinkle with chopped fresh cilantro.
9. Allow it to cool for a few minutes, then slice and serve.

Nutritional Value (Amount per Serving):

Calories: 127; Fat: 2.21; Carb: 15.86; Protein: 11.62

Sweet Italian Sausage Pizza

Prep Time: 10 Mins   Cook Time: 15 Mins   Serves: 4

Ingredients:

- 1 package Vegan Sweet Italian Sausage, sliced

- 4 cups thinly sliced bell pepper
- 2 cups thinly sliced red onion
- 1-2 jalapeño pepper, thinly sliced
- 2 garlic cloves, minced
- 4 small balls of pizza dough
- 8 oz plant-based shredded mozzarella
- 8 oz plant-based fresh mozzarella
- 1 tbsp chopped oregano
- All-purpose flour
- Olive oil
- Salt

Directions:

1. Add peppers, onion, jalapeño, garlic and oil in a bowl. Toss with salt and set aside.
2. Heat oven, put baking sheet on middle rack.
3. Stretch or roll dough until thin, about a 10-inch diameter. If sticking, dust with flour.
4. Place dough on a parchment-lined baking sheet.
5. Sprinkle each pizza with grated cheese, sliced fresh mozzarella, pepper, and onions. Arranges slices of sausage on each pizza. Sprinkle each pizza with chopped oregano.
6. Place each pizza with the parchment onto the heated baking sheet. Bake for 5-7 minutes until dough is browned, sausage is cooked and pepper and onions are slightly blackened.
7. Remove pizza from oven, place on cutting board, and cut into slices. Serve immediately.

Nutritional Value (Amount per Serving):

Calories: 866; Fat: 36.17; Carb: 71.1; Protein: 63.86

APPENDIX RECIPE INDEX

Made in the USA
Coppell, TX
29 December 2023